CALIFORNIA GOVERNMENT:

THE CHALLENGE OF CHANGE

Noel J. Stowe

GLENCOE PRESS
A division of Benziger Bruce & Glencoe, Inc.
Beverly Hills
Collier Macmillan Publishers
London

CONTENTS

PREFACE

As California moves into the second half of the 1970s, government will face a major overriding challenge—change. That is the theme of this book. The object has been to describe the various components of California government from this perspective and to show how government copes with a series of complex, ever-changing problems. The responsiveness of government to handle and hopefully to solve this continuing challenge demonstrates its ability (or inability) to function well for Californians.

In order to describe what is taking place within the government process, a rather lengthy discussion of the major issues confronting all levels of government is presented. The first two chapters set forth the basic problems, their diversity and complexity, and the solutions currently being used or discussed. Even though this book takes no position as to the correctness of any one solution, it does stress the seriousness of many issues to illustrate that solutions may be difficult to find and may have to be extreme. In subsequent chapters these subjects are briefly reexamined to demonstrate their impact on the various levels of government.

For the reader who wishes to examine any problem more closely, the footnotes suggest further reading. Most often these notes refer to articles in the *California Journal,* an excellent, objective monthly publication that reviews the state political scene in nontechnical, understandable articles. Reference to current articles will update a reader's knowledge of most issues discussed in the text.

Of course, state agencies have many *free* materials available on most of these same subjects. In a state the size of California the accessibility of a state office is remarkable. And because of that no one should hesitate to call or write a state office for information. Most offices are willing to send a wealth of information to persons interested in their activity. That is also true of the Legislature. For example, by simply writing or calling a Senator, Assemblyman, or the Clerk of the Assembly in Sacramento, any Californian may obtain a free copy of the California Constitution and a small informative book entitled *The California Legislature.* The easy availability of these materials should not be overlooked.

For the preparation of this book I am indebted to the help of several individuals. Elizabeth Schwartz aided in organizing the presentation of this book. Mae Shaw in the Governor's Office kindly and quickly provided reports and other needed information. Senator Albert S. Rodda supplied helpful criticism and observations to sharpen the discussion of many issues and to deepen my understanding of several subjects. His willingness to write the Introduction is most appreciated. Norman Barth of Sacramento City College provided valuable comments and insights on much of the text. Paul Hubbard, Associate Dean of the College of Liberal Arts, and Wallace Adams, Chairman, Department of History, at Arizona State University gave help, encouragement, and assistance so that I might see this project through to completion. Barbara Case McMahon at Glencoe Press oversaw the entire effort, gave encouragement and criticism, and aided in preparing the text in its final form. Most of all, though, I am grateful to my family for their tireless support. My wife Gwen offered invaluable comments and criticism of the writing and presentation, typed and retyped the manuscript several times, and prepared the test questions. My son Jimmy agreed to sleep through the typing, avoid playing among his father's numerous newspaper clippings, watch additional hours of Sesame Street and Electric Company, and remain cheerful through anything.

Noel J. Stowe
January, 1975

Dr. Stowe, who is a native of Sacramento, did his doctoral work at the University of Southern California. One of his fields of specialization is California and the West. Currently, he is an Associate Professor of History at Arizona State University.

INTRODUCTION

While I was teaching government, history, and economics at Sacramento City College, I became convinced that textbooks in government were too frequently so abstract and removed from reality that they lacked vitality and relevance. Dr. Noel Stowe's *California Government: The Challenge of Change* is impressive because it does not suffer from such detachment or remoteness from the realities of government and the exercise of political power. On the contrary, his work presents California government—its institutions, processes, its flexibility and adaptability in response to change—in a most meaningful and substantive manner. For this reason, students who use it as a text will benefit significantly. They will gain from their study an understanding of the subject that is dynamic and realistic, and therefore, relevant—a much-used word, but an important characteristic.

In organizing and developing his book, Dr. Stowe has done an excellent job with several difficult tasks. (1) He has provided a careful and substantial description and analysis of the structure of California's state and local government. (2) He has explained clearly the concept of the separation of powers in state government, and the role and responsibility of each branch. (3) He has delineated the historic roles and changing relationships of state and local government. (4) He has intelligently described and analyzed the political process in all of its aspects, including party structure and organization, the initiative and referendum, special interest organization and influence, the impact of the media, public relations activity, and scientific opinion polling. (5) He has constructively analyzed the meaning of representative democratic government, focusing upon the role and responsibility of individual citizens and their elected representatives as they define and implement governmental goals. (6) He has carefully analyzed the expanding function of state government as it attempts to respond to new court decisions, to the demand for greater social justice, and to the economic and environmental imperatives of contemporary society.

Underlying Dr. Stowe's discussions is a keen awareness of the gravest issue confronting the citizens of our society: whether the great problems of distributive justice, economic growth and development, environmental deterioration, public education, urban decay, and socially deviant behavior can be resolved within the framework of our present political system—one that is limited in its fiscal resources, and which must guarantee its citizens freedom from the arbitrary and abusive exercise of political power at the same time that it responds to the popular will.

As Dr. Stowe has clearly demonstrated, our society's capacity to make that guarantee will ultimately depend on the values and behavior of its citizens. If we are not familiar with the structure of representative government, and if we do not understand that democratic government must reflect enlightened (not abusive) individualism, government of the people, by the people, and for the people cannot be expected to survive.

Dr. Stowe has researched carefully and in depth the substantive issues and aspects of California state and local government. He has conscientiously observed the structure, the process, and the results of government. His work thus reveals an intimacy with and understanding of the subject which makes it a worthy contribution to instruction in California government, its history, and its present state.

Senator Albert S. Rodda
Sacramento, California
January, 1975

CHAPTER ONE

CALIFORNIA'S WORLD

Overview

This chapter stresses three basic themes: the importance of regionalism, the influence of population growth and expansion, and the role or purpose of state government. As you read, you should look for the answers to these questions:

- What are some examples of California's regionalism—cultural, political, and geographical?
- How does the state's size affect its politics?
- What has been the effect of California's being separated from the national political and economic setting?
- How has California's physical closeness to foreign countries affected her?
- What has attracted people to California?
- Where do most Californians live?
- What areas make up the "megalopolitan" setting?
- What are some of California's important ethnic and racial groups?
- What developments have helped to slow the state's growth rate?
- How does state government help to provide a uniform approach to meeting California's problems? How does state government bring unity out of the diversity that is California?

Have you ever thought of California as a *world* instead of as a state? Consider the great land area, the many different kinds of climate, and the population made up of immigrants from everywhere. Considering all that, you begin to see why California tourism pamphlets say: Visit the world . . . in California—the world within a state. Anyone who is going to understand California's government must first comprehend the tremendous variety of life in the state.

Figure 1.   Map of California

Regionalism

The State's Diversity

California's mountains, rivers, and deserts have divided it into regions that are distinct and separate. Each differs from the others in climate, natural resources, culture, and politics. This regionalism plays a significant role in the affairs of state government.

To govern such a state is much different from governing one that is made up, for example, almost entirely of plains or that has no great diversity among its people. Within the borders of California are the towering Sierra Nevada, the rugged Big Sur coast, the remote wilds of the Salmon-Trinity Alps, the historic Mother Lode, the great Central Valley, the awesome Mojave desert, cosmopolitan San Francisco, the Danish community of Solvang, and the excitement of a Hollywood set, to name only a few of the parts. Within each of these settings is a distinct life style. The state government must bring together all these different regions and make them into "one world." To consider what this truly means, let us look quickly at several areas.

Physical Isolation

One of the more isolated regions in California is the area north and east of the Cascade and Sierra Nevada mountain ranges. Within this remote corner of the state live about 30,000 people in a series of communities, the largest of which are Susanville (population 7,025) and Alturas (2,980). Economically, the area relies primarily on the sheep and beef cattle livestock industries as well as on the lumber industry.

In striking contrast to the needs and concerns of the citizens of this northeast corner of the state are those of the 7 million residents of the Los Angeles area. Defense-related industries and tourism are important economic factors here. The problems are those of a highly urban, terribly crowded area: crime, the rapidly expanding need for services, the smog, personal loss of identity, and so on.

In contrast to both of these areas is the Central Valley, a great agricultural empire of fertile soils watered by the Sacramento and San Joaquin rivers, which also includes the rich delta area. The Central Valley, making up one quarter of the state's total area, stretches as a narrow trough 450 miles in length and 50 to 60 miles in width. Some industry has been brought into the Valley, but growth remains closely tied to agriculture. Road construction and water projects are opening its previously underdeveloped west side.

Running through this great agricultural area are the rapidly growing metropolitan centers of Sacramento (875,100), Fresno (438,700), and Bakersfield (340,900). Their growth points to the eventual linking of Valley communities to form an inland tie extending south from San Francisco–Oakland to Los Angeles. The Valley's problems with which state government must deal are those of water delivery, farm labor relations, and mechanized agriculture—the problems of a rural area. But the Valley also has the problems of an expanding urban setting—race relations, ethnic politics, rapid transit, and air pollution.

The Importance of Geographical Regionalism

It is important to point out the differences between the northeastern section of the state, Los Angeles, and the Central Valley because then we can begin to understand the problems of California government. Those who govern the affairs of our state must understand the isolation of its different regions. The Cascade Mountains, the Sierra Nevada, and the Tehachapis form very real barriers between the regions despite the impact of railroads, the automobile, and the airplane. Indeed, only an unusual Californian can say he is acquainted with Tulelake, Alturas, or Susanville in the northeast, Redding, Stockton, or Delano in the central part, and Pasadena, Long Beach, or Torrance in the Los Angeles area.

Political Regionalism

To govern a state that extends a thousand miles from the Oregon border in the north to the Mexican border in the south is very different from governing a small state such as Rhode Island. The length of California covers a distance comparable to that between Maine and North Carolina, which includes *twelve* states.

The political meaning of California's vastness is illustrated in the situations of Sacramento and San Diego, two urban metropolitan centers separated by over 500 miles. To discuss the relationship of these two cities is like comparing a city in Maine with one in Virginia. Sacramento's seasonal need to control rampaging rivers seems incomprehensible to San Diego, where no rain falls sometimes for months. Both cities are part of the state's urban area, but they have little understanding or appreciation of each other's problems.

Even the voting patterns of the two areas are different. Historically, Sacramento County voters have elected Democratic candidates; San Diego has just as consistently swept into office Republicans. These voting patterns also illustrate another important reality: the traditional north–south split in California. Southern California counties are more conservatively oriented in voting for candidates and ballot measures than are the northern counties.

The north–south split visible in the state's politics also can be observed in the different overall life styles of the two regions. Southern California is well known for its casual, sun-loving style. San Franciscans are proud of their "Eastern" flavor. And neither type quite understands the other. These examples are cultural, but the political and economic regionalism is just as real, and it is partly why from time to time disputes erupt over such issues as distribution of highway funds and water resources.

National Isolation; International Closeness

Despite rail lines, highways, and airlines, California has remained in a world of its own, isolated both by physical barriers and by distance from the rest of the United States. Only since World War II has California emerged from this separateness, but the state still has remained somewhat distant from other regions. It has not been as remote with regard to other nations. The long coastline has provided access to the Pacific areas. Historically, immigration and trade have been vitally important. Immigrants from Chile, the Philippines, China, and Japan have made substantial contributions to the California setting. A joint international border with Mexico has guaranteed the continuance of an important Mexican heritage as immigrants moved north, especially during the early years of the twentieth century. The arrival of immigrants in significant numbers has meant that California maintains a distinct cosmopolitan character, both culturally and socially.

Growth and Expansion

Despite regional differences, certain issues are common to several areas of the state. Solving these problems requires of all the areas a united effort in order to build a sense of greater unity in the state as a whole. Air pollution, water pollution, and the energy crisis are examples of critical issues that are beginning to break through long-standing regional divisions, primarily because of intense population pressures.

Population Growth

Growth and expansion have been much emphasized and desired objectives in California since the 1890s. The increasing flood of people has been viewed as an indicator of greatness and prestige. In 1970, many Californians were boasting that according to that year's census, their state—third largest in physical size—was now number one in population.

In 1860, California had only 379,994 residents (about 1.2 percent of the total United States population), but in succeeding years thousands of immigrants have poured across state borders, virtually doubling the population every 20 years. By 1970, California's share of the total national population was almost 10 percent; some 19,968,004 inhabitants flooded the state, making California boosterism a spectacular success.

People come to California for a variety of reasons: climate, scenery, a more relaxed life style, outdoor living, and better employment opportunities are a few of the more important ones. By the 1960s, the flow of people into the state had reached the infamous "thousand per day." Where did these millions of people come from, and where do they reside within the state?

Growth of the Urban Population

Setting and climate have drawn most immigrants to the southern half of California. Since 1940, over half the state's growth has been in Los Angeles, San Diego, and Orange Counties. From Santa Barbara south to San Diego, vast urban areas developed. These various blossoming metropolitan areas then merged into a *megalopolis* containing well over half the state's total population. Northern California areas have grown more slowly, but the population has concentrated in a few areas, just as in the south. The major area is the San Francisco–Oakland region.

More recently, the growth rate in older metropolitan areas has slowed considerably. In the 1960s, San Francisco actually lost population; so did Los Angeles by 1971. But the populations in their surrounding areas have continued to increase, indicating that growth has simply shifted to nearby metropolitan areas. Despite this shift, growth historically has come to the state's urban areas and it has remained there.

Since 1960, California has been the nation's most urban state. By 1970, some 91 percent of her population lived in cities and suburbs. These in turn have combined to create a series of metropolitan areas which have merged into megalopolitan settings. Two centers have emerged for this vast population concentration: Los Angeles and San Francisco–Oakland. In the future, these two areas may join, linking San Francisco and San Diego together as a single vast urban unit. Here the bulk of the state's population will live on about one-third of the land area. The connecting links will be Sacramento, Stockton, Modesto, Fresno, and Bakersfield in the interior and the Monterey area along the coast. By the year 2000, this region will include some 50,000 square miles and most of California's anticipated population of 29,000,000 people.

Immigration from Other States

What is the source of the hordes of people who have poured into California? Rapid growth traditionally has come chiefly through migration rather than from a high birth rate. In the Indian, Spanish, and Mexican periods, growth was slow. Migration following Spanish colonization in 1769 was minimal and not until the 1840s did the pattern begin to change. The Anglo overland assault began in 1841 during Mexican rule and continued after California's seizure by the United States, surging forward after the discovery of gold in 1848.

By 1900, local real estate agents and developers who were originally from New England were actively promoting California. Their advertising was attracting ever-increasing numbers of middle westerners from such states as Illinois, Iowa, Ohio, and Missouri. And by the 1930s, Dust Bowl immigrants were joining them. Important racial and ethnic groups also were coming in significant numbers. Blacks began arriving after 1910 and by the 1940s, Los Angeles had become a major Black population center in the nation.[1]

Immigration from Other Cultures

To these migrants were added those of other nations. Mexicans were attracted to the state; especially large and important groups entered during the 1920s and early 1940s. By the 1970s, over 16 percent of the population was Mexican-American. Los Angeles has the state's largest Mexican community—indeed, the largest such community outside of Mexico City and Guadalajara. In the second and third decades of this century, smaller numbers of Japanese immigrants arrived to settle permanently. Los Angeles has also become a major center for the Japanese, with the community of Little Tokyo flourishing in the heart of Los Angeles. Filipinos and Chinese also arrived from Asia. The Chinese immigrants came in two groups—the first in the mid-nineteenth century, and the second following World War II. They developed major communities in San Francisco and Los Angeles. Other foreign immigrants such as the Portuguese came in lesser numbers. The cumulative result of all this influx is that California today is one of the nation's most cosmopolitan settings (see Figure 2).

Figure 2.   California's Minority Group Population—1970

Minority Group	Total Numbers	Percentages
Mexican-Americans*	3,101,589	16
Blacks	1,397,138	7
Japanese	212,121	1
Chinese	170,374	0.9
Filipinos	135,641	0.7
Indians	88,271	0.4
Koreans	16,648	0.08

*This figure (which is the one most often cited) actually refers to the Spanish Language/Spanish Surname population. It is impossible to estimate accurately California's Mexican American population because the 1970 census did not ask for that information. In that census, however, 411,008 people did identify themselves as Mexican-born and 701,000 as of Mexican descent, a total of 1,112,008.

Two things should be noted about California's immigrants. First, they have contributed to the great growth and expansion of the state. Second, they have flowed from all parts of the world and from all segments of the United States. California's population has never been a single social-cultural unit but a vital mixture.

Today's Declining Growth Rate

By 1964, the pattern of migration had begun to change. Annual migration declined; fewer people were coming to California, and more were leaving than in previous years. As a result, future growth is likely to be less spectacular, and, for the first time, to be tied more closely to the birth rate. Because the state's birth rate also has been declining, it appears that the period of tremendous population growth is at an end. Even though projections are for a continuing rise in the state's population, that increase will be much smaller.

Why has the immigration rate begun to stabilize for the first time since the middle of the nineteenth century? What has happened is that the flood of people who came helped to change—to destroy the very things that lured immigrants here—the climate, the scenery, and the outdoor living. Open spaces have disappeared. Today, going to a southern California beach is a private war between several thousand people who jostle for space in the polluted water, step over the garbage on the beach, and strain to see the blue sky through an unhealthy layer of smog. By 1970, the employment setting of California had become bleak. Aerospace and defense cutbacks had adversely affected the job market and unemployment was high. Highly skilled and educated scientists, engineers, and technicians found themselves without jobs, and highly trained new college graduates were no longer being snapped up by waiting employers.

In short, California had lost her innocence. Quite simply, the problems newcomers thought that they had left behind they actually brought with them. California's urban centers become daily more like those of the East which the immigrants had fled.

The Role of California Government

The issues the state government of California faces in the 1970s are basically the result of the great numbers of people living in the state. Who will confront these problems? How will they be solved? Because of their vastness and complexity, California needs an effective, powerful state government. Air pollution and energy-related problems, for example, only can be dealt with through statewide attack. Local government can implement the broader policies in their own areas, but state government is the only agency that can mount the necessary unified statewide effort.

Government as a Process

California's government consists of three branches, and a series of institutions fills out the structure. That can all be diagrammed on an organizational chart, but government must be thought of as more than just a structure. It is a procedure or *process* in action. In a state as large as California, where so many different groups live, and so many different interests exist, it is vital to see government as a process in which the will of the majority is expressed in political power. It is equally important to keep in mind that this process will function well only so long as it remains open and alert to the minority. Thus, the majority and minority must both remain sensitive to one another, neither attempting to impose its will exclusively.

Government as a Source of Unity in the State.   As you read about California government's efforts to meet the issues facing the state, it is important to recall the concept of government as a process at work. In order to solve problems many varied opinions must be gathered for review. The resulting answers should reflect the majority public interest and needs. To bring unity out of diversity, these needs must be met. If not, and if minority and special interests prevail, diversity will split the state into multiple segments.[2]

What Governing Means

The procedure of governing must be thought of as including various active elements: making decisions; examining, allocating, and developing resources; forming, reviewing, and changing policies; setting new priorities and pushing aside outdated ones; selecting new directions from a variety of possible courses of action; planning for present and future needs.

In carrying out these functions, the governing process affects each individual and his or her social and physical environments. Thus, it is important that the process be open, sensitive, flexible, and responsive to changes in public interest and needs. Then government's goal of unity can be at least somewhat successfully won as it faces the challenging problems of the 1970s.[3]

Review Questions

What is the influence of diversity and isolation on California politics?

What might be the differences between the problems of the megalopolis, and those of "ordinary" urban areas?

Where have California's immigrants come from?

What does it mean to say that government is a process?

Notes

1. Gerald D. Nash, *The American West in the Twentieth Century: A Short History of An Urban Oasis* (Englewood Cliffs, N.J.: Prentice-Hall, 1973), pp. 13–16, 77–78, 148–153, 197–199. Gerald Nash has an interesting discussion of the various groups who migrated and how they became interested in California.

2. Albert S. Rodda, "Essential Meanings of Democracy," *California Elementary Administrator* 31 (May–June, 1968): 25–26.

3. Heinz Eulan and Kenneth Prewitt, *Labyrinths of Democracy: Adaptations, Linkages, Representation, and Policies in Urban Politics* (Indianapolis: Bobbs-Merrill Co., 1973), pp. 16–17.

CHAPTER TWO

A WORLD OF ISSUES

Overview

This chapter reviews some of the most important issues and situations challenging California government. From reading about each one you should learn:

- What is the problem and what are its key elements?
- Which groups have a special interest and what is their interest?
- What solutions have been proposed and who proposed them?
- What government agency or board is involved?
- What plan or law has been put into effect?

Californians are faced with many problems that relate to the quality of life in the state. Among these are transportation planning, the energy crisis, diminishing federal funds, tax reform, adequate school financing, ethnic politics, and a whole range of environmental concerns—air pollution, water distribution and quality, coastal preservation, and land use.

Air Pollution

Environmental quality—when and how did the decline set in? What are the sources of pollution? Quite simply, Californians have constructed a series of facilities and pursued a series of activities that have had unforeseen side effects. Smog-filled skies come from pouring massive amounts of wastes into the atmosphere each day. Open burning, incinerators, industries, power plants, motor vehicles, and airplanes are the most common violators. Until recently, smog was identified exclusively with southern California and the Los Angeles basin. Central Valley residents refused to call their haze by its proper label. Now it is painfully obvious that all California communities experience some degree of pollution. The larger the community, the worse the problem, but such diverse cities as Eureka, Redding, San Francisco, Santa Rosa, Salinas, and Visalia all must deal with it.

Smog: Its Causes and Effects

Clearly, smog affects the quality of life—it damages, impairs, and destroys. The expanding pollution output is the result of urbanization, industrialization, and an affluent society. Greater wealth has brought more electrical appliances and automobiles. To run these appliances, more pollutant-producing power plants have been built. Increased car use has produced more gases to create more smog.

One of the more curious aspects of California's smog is that it in part results from the natural environment and climate that have attracted people and industry. California air pollution is photochemical smog caused by the reaction of oxides of nitrogen and hydrocarbons (from cars, industries, and other sources) combined with sunlight. The major smog season extends from mid-spring through fall during the period of clear, warm, dry weather with relatively low wind. This weather results from temperature inversion, a layer of warm air overlying cooler air at the surface, and is ideal for trapping and holding pollution near its source. The photochemical reaction produces compounds that reduce visibility and irritate the eyes, nose, and throat; damage plant life; and produce cracking rubber and peeling paint. Plant damage occurs in over half the state's counties at a cost of almost $26 million in 1970 alone. By late 1973, crop damage resulting from smog totaled $95 million for the previous four-year period. In November 1973, the lettuce crop in Orange County was almost completely wiped out by an unknown air pollutant. Spinach is no longer grown in many areas of southern California, and citrus, lettuce, and vegetables grown there suffer severely. Smog also has damaged over half the Ponderosa pines in the San Bernardino National Forest 60 miles away from Los Angeles.

Air Resources Board

Choking Californians often ask, who is in charge of air pollution control? The task is spread over several federal, state, and local agencies. The basic California agency to control air pollution and enforce the Clean Air Act passed by Congress is the Air Resources Board (ARB) created in 1967 to draw together the functions of previous agencies. Figure 3 lists some of its important activities and duties.

The work of the ARB is based on the idea that the state should review and evaluate local controls, provide technical assistance, and act where local measures are insufficient. One of its fundamental tasks is to put pressure on local air pollution control districts to function more effectively.

Figure 3.   Air Resources Board (ARB)

The ARB was created in 1967 by the Mulford–Carrell Air
Resources Act, as California's primary agent in the battle against
air pollution. Its duties include the following:

Studies cause and effect, and develops solutions.
- Administers and coordinates a program of air pollution research.
- Conducts studies of the causes of air pollution, and its effects
  on human, plant, and animal life.
- Tests and approves vehicle emission control devices.

*Coordinates the activities of local air pollution control districts
(APCDs).*

*Organizes the state into a series of "air basins" for pollution
control purposes.*

Sets and enforces emissions standards.
- Adopts standards for ambient air quality in each "air basin."
- Sets emission standards for all nonvehicular sources of air
  pollution for each "air basin."
- Sets standards for exhaust emissions from new and used motor
  vehicles, and enforces them.
- Regulates agricultural, range, forest, and open-dump burning.

Hard Decisions for the 1970s

The 1970s require stricter and more radical antipollution measures than
those employed thus far, which have affected the average Californian
little, if at all. For example, until recently the auto industry assumed rising
antipollution expenses as part of production costs and did not pass them
on fully to the customer. Now, even used cars must be equipped with
owner-supplied antismog devices. Also, public transit must be expanded
at significant cost to the taxpayer.

In early 1973, the federal Environmental Protection Agency (EPA)
was forced to recognize the ineffectiveness of either the ARB or local
air pollution control districts in meeting the clean air requirements for
Los Angeles. The EPA suggested gas rationing to cut gasoline consumption
by up to 82 percent during the worst smog months. In southern California
over 6 million cars would be affected.

From the clamor of the opposition that greeted this suggestion, it was obvious that Californians wanted their automobiles to remain free from controls as long as possible. But it was equally evident that there were painful choices to be made and carried through if clean air were ever to reappear over southern California or elsewhere in the state. Communities such as Bakersfield, Modesto, Stockton, Fresno, and Sacramento were startled to discover that the air crisis affected them too and that if gas rationing were going to be applied to Los Angeles, it would be applied to them as well.

Opposition to the severe suggestions of the EPA was making headway by late 1973, however, as oil supplies rapidly diminished and the energy crisis took hold. Unfortunately, most EPA suggestions increased fuel consumption or prohibited the use of some fuel sources in order to meet air standards. Congress began reviewing the Clean Air Act in order to change the 1977 deadline that had been set. Suggestions even were made to delay the clean air deadlines by five to ten years. However, it was quite clear that these were to be delays, not an abandonment of the standards.

To apply these standards will require an altered life style. The simple fact is that cars have to be driven less. State and local agencies face the task of forcing people out of their cars, off the freeways, into public transit, and into car pools. Also, costlier pollution control devices must be added to new and used cars, and cleaner electric power generation must be required. Restrictions on traffic in certain areas or during certain times will have to come. The cost to Californians will be higher taxes, changes in habits, and perhaps even moves closer to work. These costs are high, but the benefits should be correspondingly great.[1]

Transportation Needs

Closely tied to the problem of air pollution are mass transportation needs and problems, for both urban and rural areas of the state. Planners are faced with commuter problems, increased air travel, greater noise pollution, and expanded highway use. The task now is to form plans for a balanced transportation setting—the most sensible, economical, feasible, and efficient movement of goods and people. Land use, air pollution, and noise problems must be balanced with transportation requirements. The cause and effect relationship between transportation recommendations and the natural as well as social and economic environments needs careful study.

California's approach to transportation has been an almost total commitment to motor vehicles. By 1972, over $1.5 billion a year was being invested in road construction, and at the state level alone some 18,000 people devoted their time to highway work. California first began a state highway system in 1895, but the real growth came following the passage of two legislative acts. First, the 1947 Collier–Burns Act revised the gas tax to provide needed construction money and forced added road construction responsibilities upon the state. Second, the Legislature approved a master plan for a statewide freeway-expressway system in 1959.

Public Attitude Changes

Orginally, the emphasis on road building received enthusiastic and almost overwhelming support. However, by the mid-1960s mixed feelings about freeways were noticeable and by the 1970s there was open hostility. While the majority of Californians are not opposed to freeways, they have been astounded by what seems to be an almost ruthless planning of routings, and the huge, ugly structures that often have resulted. The agency responsible for all this was the California Highway Commission, an almost totally independent body.

By 1965, enough resistance had surfaced to force changes. For example, the legal provision requiring the Highway Commission to adopt the "most direct and practical location" for routings was dropped so that alternate, less destructive routes could be used. By 1972, Commission requirements demanded studies of effects on ecology, agricultural and environmental values, and noise as a part of highway planning. However, by the time the Commission was requiring these studies and examining the influence of road building on environmental quality, 3,197 miles of freeways were already in use. Greater restrictions on planning and construction will come, however, as a result of rapidly rising costs and the withdrawal of areas from planning. For example, the coastline was withdrawn from freeway planning in 1971 in an effort to preserve its uniqueness.[2]

Rising concern over environmental quality also is forcing more serious study of transit systems. While the Los Angeles area limps along with the inadequate bus system of the Southern California Rapid Transit District (SCRTD)—its most creative efforts were the use of a few experimental steam-powered and gas-powered buses, special freeway lanes, and reduced bus fares—most of the state's attention is focused on the operation of the Bay Area Rapid Transit (BART). BART marks California's first major effort to return to mass transit since automobile use destroyed earlier transit operations in the state. Despite BART's cost (over $1.4 billion), size (75 miles), and hope to include interlinking lines to areas as distant as Sacramento, the system is not really total enough to be called mass transit. It will not carry enough commuters, nor include enough of the Bay Area, and may cause further population growth, thus offsetting any gains. And already it has faced serious financial problems. Yet, it remains the single major new mass transit effort in the state, and it may signal the start of other such programs.[3]

A basic problem still remains for all transit systems: how to remove Californians from their cars. Buses are unattractive—costs for better systems are high. Yet more stringent air quality standards eventually may force limited use of cars, require gas rationing, and close some areas to traffic, thereby forcing Californians to use the presently inadequate systems and to pay for the construction of efficient ones. Californians now may be cautious in their support of freeways, but they seem unready to give up their automobiles.

Some powerful state groups still support freeways. Their continued interest has been evident every time measures appear before the Legislature or voters (for instance, Proposition 18 in 1970) to rechannel some gas tax revenues towards financing transit systems and motor vehicle pollution control. Auto clubs, oil companies, the California Chamber of Commerce, contractors, and others have provided intense, well-financed opposition to such suggestions.

The gasoline shortages in 1973 and 1974 greatly helped to force Californians to recognize the need for alternate transportation planning. The June 1974 ballot once again carried a proposal, Proposition 5, to permit part of the gas tax revenues to be funneled into rapid transit development. This time the measure was approved. Up to $50 million a year is to be invested in non-highway transportation development, and the availability of these state funds will bring in additional federal money.

Multimodal Transportation
and the Department of Transportation

For transportation, the key word of the 1970s is *multimodal.* Transportation planning must include several modes, or types, of travel, rapid transit for one. We can no longer rely on only one mode—highways and freeways. A web of transportation facilities and services needs developing.

To provide new direction and to plan a multimodal approach a Department of Transportation (Cal Trans) was established, and began operating on July 1, 1973. Now the emphasis is on regional planning and the use of regional agencies to develop local area plans with the help of the new state department. By drawing together these local and regional plans, a California Transportation Plan can be created for presentation to the State Legislature in January 1976. The plan is to take into consideration environmental and social conditions, proper land use, non-highway-oriented solutions, citizen participation, and the expansion of existing modes. It is to be developed by Cal Trans under the supervision of the State Transportation Board—an independent body serving to advise both the Legislature and the Business and Transportation Agency, under which Cal Trans functions.

For the portions of California as yet untouched by urban sprawl, the major transportation concern relates to recreational travel. Elaborate self-contained vehicles pulling dune buggies or carrying boats or trail bikes are invading all areas. Even campgrounds and narrow rural highways in previously remote areas are crowded. Parking lot culture is creeping into more sections than ever before with an assault as serious as that required for a freeway, and as destructive. Yet, this remains one of the more unrecognized aspects of the California transportation setting, perhaps because it represents the latest way to pursue the old ideal of outdoor living.

Land Use Problems

Land Use and Misuse

Because of California's population growth, land use in both rural and urban areas is under increasing study. While the period of exploding growth is at an end, the population will still increase. Thus, urban expansion, travel, and road building will continue. Communities will find themselves forced to extend services into areas where costs for these services will far exceed income. More agricultural lands and wildlife areas will be destroyed. Farms will appear on less fertile land, and wildlife breeding and feeding habits will be disrupted. Already the southern California citrus industry has been tremendously decreased as a result of the construction of homes and shopping centers. Orchards in the Santa Clara Valley have disappeared. Even the Napa wine vineyards are headed for similar problems. This problem of changing land use coupled with the dismal effects of air pollution on crops has created major problems for the state's major industry. In the long run, the loss of the most valuable fertile areas of the state to urban development threatens the ability of California agriculture to produce and harvest the crops for which it is so famous. Homes, stores, and roads are encroaching not only on farmlands, but also on foothill and mountain sectors previously unspoiled by urban "conveniences."

The basic issue here is the most suitable and most proper use of land, which increasingly is being considered as an irreplaceable natural resource. This new attitude is truly remarkable because Californians have for so long looked upon land as something to be "developed" for its maximum possible use and greatest market value. Thus, coastline areas have been destroyed, prime farmland overrun, and cities subjected to even more concentrated development.

To discourage this tendency, environmentalists increasingly advocate governmental action *before* public and private projects wipe out still more valuable areas. The change in direction emerged in the mid-1960s with the passage in 1965 of the California Land Conservation Act (Williamson Act) and voters' approval of a constitutional addition on "Open Space Conservation" (Article 28, November 1966). The Land Conservation Act provides a way for owners to escape high taxes for maintaining agricultural land, admitting the need and desirability of maintaining and conserving open spaces. While critics said that both measures raised more problems than they solved, the state through its Legislature and citizens had begun to acknowledge a concern over suitable land use.

Environmental Quality Act

Perhaps it was the 1970 Environmental Quality Act (EQA) that fully involved the state in the whole issue of land development. The significance of the EQA was its requirement that environmental impact reports be filed for all construction projects that might have a significant effect on the environment. It was originally unclear whether or not private projects were included under the act. In Mono County at the resort of Mammoth, a private organization planned the construction of a series of multistoried condominiums, shops, and other facilities. After the project received approval from the Board of Supervisors, a group of Mammoth residents banded together as the Friends of Mammoth to block the development, contending that it would have significant undesirable effects on the area's environment. In September 1972, the State Supreme Court decided in favor of the Friends, and most important, determined that private projects *were* included under the EQA.

During the same month, a Court of Appeal also said that state courts might decide if submitted environmental impact reports were in fact adequate. Quickly following the state Supreme Court's decision, the Legislature acted to include that decision in the law by requiring cities and counties to file impact reports. In December 1972, this legislation became law. The EQA, the *Friends of Mammoth* ruling, and the following legislative action pointed to a new trend in thinking about land development and seemed to indicate that the days of unplanned and uncontrolled growth have ended.[4]

Use of Restricted Zoning

Another drive to regulate land use involves zoning classifications, in an effort to control land use as well as to prevent certain types of development. For instance, zoning decisions by the Tahoe Regional Planning Agency to force low-density development, and by the City of Palo Alto to force open space requirements in its foothill area ended up in the courts. Land holders are charging that their Fifth Amendment rights are being violated, that their property has been taken without just compensation because they cannot develop it as they want to.

Other examples of new zoning philosophies exist. San Francisco, much concerned about newly built, multistoried buildings changing the character of the city, adopted a plan in 1972 to limit building size and bulk in balance with other considerations—primarily setting: the need for openness, the need to preserve and reuse older structures for new purposes, the effort to guard a special cultural and social feeling in each area.

Preservation of Open Space

What is open space? It is land that contains few if any buildings, that provides relief, variety, or protection: golf courses, open marshlands, cemeteries, agricultural land, parks, wildlife refuges, flood plains, earthquake fault zones, open airport runway corridors. Some such space is held open for safety reasons, some for future development, and some for recreational use. It is open for a purpose, and is not therefore considered "undeveloped."

The tendency in urban areas is toward development and thus the elimination of open space. The destruction of the coastline in Los Angeles County through overuse—Malibu, for instance—is a good illustration. Plans to "develop" the Santa Monica mountains—by virtually leveling them—fortunately have been met with much resistance. Open space can be valuable in separating land segments of conflicting usage, preserving a desirable community feeling, or providing recreation.

The governments of Los Angeles and Sacramento, and others are actively involved in attempts to preserve scenic beauty and maintain open spaces for the future. In these as well as all urban areas, what *not* to develop is the problem.

San Francisco Bay Conservation and Development Commission. One of the earliest and most remarkable efforts to preserve open space and to regulate land use to the most suitable development is in the work of the San Francisco Bay Conservation and Development Commission (BCDC). It was first created in 1965, and established permanently in 1969 to protect the Bay, prevent its being filled and becoming even more polluted, and plan the best use of bay shore lands. In 1969, the Commission produced a comprehensive plan to accomplish these and other goals, and it has since moved ahead to realize them.

Coastline Preservation. The effort to preserve the entire 1,000-mile-long California coastline is one of the best examples of a campaign for proper land use. In November 1972, California voters approved a direct initiative measure, providing for a more orderly approach to coastline development. A California Coastal Zone Conservation Commission was established along with six regional commissions. Treating the coast as a valuable natural resource, the Coastal Zone Conservation Act requires the commissions to draw up a plan for presentation to the Legislature by December 1975. Figure 4 indicates some of the major points the plan is to cover. In the meantime, the State Commission and the six regional commissions must approve all development along the coast. They will do so until the Act expires in 1976, to be replaced by the adoption of the plan.

While similar in outlook to the San Francisco BCDC, the coastal zone idea is broader and shows the current concern for development in the 1970s. Development within certain limits, or no development at all seem to be the ideas now uppermost in Californians' thinking. In terms of the coastal idea, a balancing of needs—a conservation development balance—must be achieved, if the entire coast is not to be ruined. The

---

Figure 4.

The California Coastal Zone Conservation Plan is to be prepared by the Commission with the aid of the six regional commissions, and submitted to the Legislature by December 1, 1975. It is to be based on detailed studies of all factors affecting the zone. It is to accomplish the following aims:

- To define precisely, comprehensively, the public interest in the coastal zone.
- To contain ecological planning principles and assumptions to be used in determining the suitability and the extent of development.
- To include recommendations on:

  land use
  transportation
  conservation of scenic/
     natural resources
  public services (power
     plants)
  education/scientific use

  recreation
  maximum population
     densities
  ocean mineral and living
     resources
  public access for visual
     and physical use

- To suggest reservation of land or water for certain use or the prohibition of using land or water in specific areas.
- To recommend the governmental policies and powers needed to carry out the plan and to suggest the organization and authority of the agency to assume permanent responsibility for the plan.

coastal effort marks the first statewide attempt to use governmental power to upgrade, protect, or develop the quality of the environment, and it may signal a broader trend for more such plans. It also indicates a trend toward using regional agencies—the level between community and state—a new idea in government to deal more effectively with broad-area needs.[5]

Awakened Interest in Land Use Legislation

Voter approval of the coastline commissions and the Legislature's passage of the EQA clearly reveal a growing acceptance of land use planning. This is true not only on the state level but nationally as well. In the early 1970s, Congress undertook serious reviews of land use planning and management proposals to encourage the states to provide substantial funding for that work.

At the same time, the California Legislature was reviewing possible legislation to coordinate state and local laws on land management, agricultural and urban policy, and land planning. In order to overcome the confusion of local laws and policies, the proposed legislation made land use planning a state responsibility. A state planning council was also under discussion.

Pressure to require better land use was coming from both inside and outside the state. In addition, the activity of the Air Resources Board, the Water Resources Control Board (to be discussed later), and the federal Environmental Protection Agency focused more attention on the overall environmental effects of land use. For example, air pollution obviously can be lessened by limiting certain kinds of development that encourage it. Even though the Air Resources Board was hesitating about limiting such types of new construction, the federal EPA did not. Under the authority of the federal Clean Air Act, in 1973 and 1974 the EPA began drawing up restrictions for new shopping centers and parking lots. In fact, the first related court action under the Clean Air Act involved a group of private citizens who were attempting to block shopping center and parking lot construction in Arcadia on the grounds that it would prevent their area from achieving and maintaining clean air standards.

A strong, aroused interest in land use ideas has emerged. New environmental legislation to force coordinated planning at the state level and to bring order to land use planning and policies at the local level seems an immediate possibility.[6]

California Water Needs

Just as Californians' approach to land use has matured, so also has their thinking about water development. As a result of climatic differences between northern and southern California, more than two-thirds of the state's water supply has always occurred north of Sacramento, while southern California's economic development—stimulated partly by its sunny climate—creates more than two-thirds of the state's water demand south of Sacramento. Years ago, to solve this problem, southern Californians began looking beyond their area for added water. The Owens Valley development was an early major part of that effort. Use of Colorado River water came later as did suggestions to do to northern California what had been done previously to the Owens Valley—seize the water of that area for the needs of the larger growing area. A California Water Plan was put together in the decade following 1947, and authorized in 1957, with the goal of studying the state's water resources and recommending future usage.

State Water Project

One of the first steps in developing the Plan was the formulation of the State Water Project, basically a mammoth undertaking to move northern California's water south. The Project was to benefit the Bay area and other coastal segments, as well as deliver water to the extremely dry west side of the San Joaquin Valley to encourage new development, and to provide water to the thirsty Los Angeles and San Diego areas.

Several aspects of the Project proved to be controversial—cost was one. Critics said the cost might be from two to five times the original estimate. The ecology of the Delta was another issue. Water was to flow south toward the Sacramento–San Joaquin Delta, where it was to be intercepted by a peripheral canal for the transfer south. Critics charged that if the project were carried out, the necessary amount of water might not be allocated to preserve fish and wildlife in the Delta and to combat salt water incursion. Would that needed water be transported south instead, and cut off from Delta use by the peripheral canal?

Diverting North Coastal Rivers. An additional problem was the intended raid on north coast rivers. The huge Oroville Dam on the Feather River (originally referred to as the Feather River Project) was the key to the water supply of the system, but more water was needed for future use. That water was to be secured by damming the Eel, Klamath, Trinity, and other rivers and sending their waters east into the Sacramento system for delivery to the peripheral canal and Delta for transfer southward. A fantastic run-off pours—rages—through these north coastal rivers, often flooding surrounding areas. Experts felt that flood control and water redistribution were therefore needed, but critics of the Project defended the unspoiled wild nature of these rivers as worthy of preservation. They wanted no "development" of the rivers, or at most, limited development for local purposes. A "Committee of Two Million" soon appeared to support and win the Wild Rivers legislation fight of 1972, generally halting dam construction on those north coast rivers.

The Peripheral Canal Issue

That the support for huge water projects has ended is evidenced in the strong resistance to the peripheral canal, in support for the preservation of Delta ecology, and in the successful drive to achieve the Wild Rivers legislation. Indeed, the entire California Water Project was under heavy criticism by 1973 when Governor Ronald Reagan somewhat prematurely dedicated the Project's completion. While this actually marked only the completion of the first phase, additional dams and aqueducts were being planned, and were needed to fulfill the total project. Environmentalists, though, were making an all-out attack, contending the Project never should have been started. Their basic argument against the Project was that it spoiled the landscape from its point of origin in northern California all along its 444 mile-long length.

The future held further disaster, they argued, because if completed, the Project would trigger unrestrained urbanization and land development all along the aqueduct, especially in the south, thereby creating a greater water shortage! Clearly, they said, to prevent more damage to the state, the Project must cease additional construction. To stop the building of the peripheral canal became the immediate target. If it could be stopped, the entire Project would be in jeopardy, because its goals in terms of water delivery could never be accomplished without that canal or the use of the Delta.

Defenders of the Project claimed that the canal was planned to preserve the Delta's quality, and that the Delta that environmentalists were trying to save was not a natural phenomenon. It was created in the twentieth century, they said, by water releases from Shasta Dam and other projects (supplying a steady water flow and preventing salt water incursion), and from modern levee construction.

New Trends in Water Planning

Other plans besides the California Water Project were also under fire. In the 1970s, strong forces insisted that environmental impact be considered first, or at least on an equal footing, with other results of proposed projects. The era of single-minded project development was past. Alternative planning was the new approach. The newest task of water management was to balance two sides of an equation: the needs and desires for flood control and water supply for industry, communities, or agriculture, or hydroelectric production versus the needs for preservation of fish and wildlife, recreation, open space, wild rivers, and scientific and historic values. More than ever before, water planning was to be people-oriented rather than product-oriented.

Major, large-scale water project planning had ended. New plans would be smaller in scope, and probably would focus more on ground water management, geothermal sources, desalinization of both ocean water and brackish agricultural waste water. Another emphasis would be on the reclamation and recycling of waste water, such as has been going on at Golden Gate Park, Whittier Narrows, Santee, Pomona, and Oceanside. One reason this shift could be accomplished was the reduction in the growth rate of California's population. This meant current projects could adequately supply needs longer and that more alternatives could be considered for future development. In total though, it was clear that massive projects would no longer be the California way.[7]

Porter–Cologne
Water Quality Control Act

The quality of water has not always been considered such a major issue in California as its quantity. Efforts to combat pollution really first appeared following 1949. In the late 1960s, the focus shifted to quality, with the effort to ensure an organized approach to water quality management. In 1969, in response to a study made on water quality and pollution, the Legislature enacted the Porter–Cologne Water Quality Control Act, which became effective in 1970.

Many people believe this act to be an extremely strong one. In establishing it, the Legislature set forth the state's position on water quality, stressing primary interest in the conservation, control, and utilization of water resources, as well as an interest in protecting the "quality of all the waters of the state" for use and enjoyment. Regulating the state's waters "to attain the highest water quality which is reasonable" is also of major importance. All demands placed on state water resources are to be considered and noted in achieving the highest quality—that is, demands that are "beneficial and detrimental, economic and social, tangible and intangible."

The group charged with securing water quality is a State Water Resources Control Board (SWRCB), along with nine California Regional Water Quality Control Boards. The SWRCB retains final authority over the regional boards, so that a statewide framework, policy, and policing of quality will be assured. The regional boards are to confront the tremendous diversity of local water quality problems, gearing their work to area needs, requirements, and solutions, and encouraging public participation.

Basically then, Porter–Cologne established a regional government approach to handle water quality; the statewide effort through the SWRCB is mainly a matter of coordination.

Land use—present and future—population growth, and agriculture and industrial development are some of the items to be considered in developing regional plans. In addition, both the socioeconomic and environmental impacts of the quality plans are to be evaluated. The task of putting together and enforcing regional plans will be tremendous, but supporters feel water quality will be assured.

On the other hand, critics felt the whole Porter–Cologne Act needed upgrading. They charged that because polluters had been represented among the group that formulated the Act, it was uncertain whether or not the Boards and their plans actually could be effective. Polluters had a great many ways of avoiding compliance, they charged—for example, under the procedures of the Act, it actually would take some time to halt pollution from a given source. In addition, agricultural pollution is not covered, and the ongoing careful collection of water quality information so essential for planning and enforcement has been a process very slow in starting.

What the critics overlooked was that, in the face of much potential opposition, the Porter–Cologne Act was passed without much difficulty. Why? Because both the potential violators and environmentalists had helped to form it. It represented much negotiation and compromise, and as a result moved rather easily through the Legislature. While the Act certainly could have been strengthened, that can be done in future years. It is remarkable, really, that water quality was declared important enough for the Act to pass.[8]

Water Quality Is Expensive

What can an emphasis on water quality mean? For the Regional Board of Los Angeles it meant special concern for a 27-mile stretch of coastline. This Board was interested in designating the coast from Malibu north to Mugu Lagoon as an Area of Special Biological Significance. If this idea were to be adopted, it would mean water discharges into the ocean would have to be free of chemicals or would have to be halted entirely. For Santa Barbara it meant a continuing dispute with both the Regional Board and the Attorney General's office over an ancient sewage treatment plant—a dispute that could result in a ban on new building construction until the plant was upgraded, plus a heavy daily fine for continued pollution. For Sacramento, it meant a massive overhaul of sewage facilities to meet the demands of the Central Valley Water Quality Control Board. To meet the cost of such a project, Sacramento voters approved a $75 million bond issue in June 1974, to meet their share of a new $240 million sewer system.

Obviously, then, water quality will be costly, and the development of adequate facilities may be slow. Furthermore, because industries tying into sewage systems will have to bear a major proportion of the cost, based upon their total discharge into the system, they might well consider moving their plants to avoid such costs. Water quality control, therefore, is affected by many of the factors raised in the previous discussion on land use planning.

Energy Crisis

One of the most serious environmental problems to emerge in the 1970s is the energy crisis. While this issue had been discussed since the late 1960s, it was only in 1973 that it became an immediate problem. At that time, it seemed that unless definite action were taken, Californians would soon experience electricity brownouts and blackouts and a severe lack of gasoline.

What was the problem? By 1973, natural gas supplies to California public utility or power companies were declining. Because these companies used natural gas to run their generating plants to produce electricity, they had to find other means of producing electricity. However, they were unable to use coal rather than natural gas, because of air pollution restrictions. The use of oil was also severely restricted: only low-sulphur oil could be used, because of its low air pollution characteristics.

Environmental Restrictions

Also complicating the situation were restrictions on new oil drilling off the California coastline in the Santa Barbara area. The environmental danger to marine life and to the coastline from oil spills had caused the state to close these fields. The federal government also had greatly restricted development of offshore oil in areas under its control. Thus, not only was the use of oil restricted, but the production of oil also was curtailed, causing a shortage.

To overcome these problems, power companies were attempting to construct nuclear power plants, but they were blocked here as well, because of environmental reasons. One was a problem of site selection—where to locate such a plant so that it was unlikely to be severely damaged during an earthquake. Another issue involved the fact that great quantities of water must be used to cool the nuclear core. Power companies wanted to use ocean water for this purpose. Environmentalists objected, arguing that dumping warm water back into the ocean would destroy the ecology of that area. Furthermore, what was to be done with the radioactive waste from a nuclear power plant? Where was it to be stored? Would any nearby population be safe from contamination?

Environmentalists were not satisfied with public utilities' answers to these questions. Power companies' efforts to increase the generation of electricity were severely handicapped because of such rising environmental concerns. On the other hand, environmentalists had found that more and more Californians were concerned with the quality of life and their environment. Legislative passage of the Wild Rivers Act and voter approval of the California Coastal Conservation Act showed the rising importance and power of environmentalist groups. By 1973, when the energy crisis emerged as a major issue, environmentalists had never been in a stronger position to have a say in the solution of that crisis.

The 1973–74 Winter Energy Crisis

What brought the energy crisis out into the open? The first major trigger was a gasoline shortage. In the spring and early summer of 1973, major oil refineries announced that they would be unable to meet the gasoline needs of the nation. Oil companies began rationing the distribution of their gasoline. There was a serious shortage not only of gasoline for cars, but also of oil to run electric generators. These shortages actually revealed the much larger problem of a total energy crisis.

By August and September, the situation had worsened. Both major suppliers of electricity to southern California, the city-owned Los Angeles Department of Water and Power and Southern California Edison, predicted they would be unable to meet electricity demands in 1974. The Department of Water and Power believed that blackouts would have to be imposed as early as March 1974. Then in October 1973, the Arab nations ordered a curtailment of all shipments of oil from their areas. This sudden decrease in the availability of foreign oil, on top of already diminished oil sources in California and the rest of the United States, caused an immediate energy crisis. By the end of the year, office and home heating had been reduced, outdoor lighting was restricted, the speed limit had been reduced, gasoline stations were limiting sales, and gas rationing was being discussed. Customers of the Department of Water and Power in Los Angeles faced severe rate increases and the threat of shut-offs if they did not decrease their use of energy. Southern California in particular was heavily dependent on oil imports from Saudi Arabia and so felt the crunch more than some other regions of the state.

By the spring of 1974, the energy crisis seemed to be slowly lifting. The situation remained serious, but the flow of oil from the Middle East had begun to increase. The energy problem, however, had been clearly identified, and now measures would have to be seriously considered to try to avoid a repeat of the 1973–74 crisis.

The problem of meeting the energy crisis has two parts. First, energy production must be expanded. Second, as that expansion occurs, the environment must be protected. How to accomplish both goals is a crisis in itself. Californians have grown accustomed to having their increasing energy needs met by the power utilities; now, because of the problems of generating more electricity, some critics say the public's demands for energy will have to be reduced.

Many suggestions have been made as to how this reduction could be accomplished. Gasoline rationing, car pools, reduced speed limits, and greater use of rapid transit have been recommended. Another suggestion is that gas pilot lights be eliminated on new appliances. Builders must be required to use more insulation in constructing new buildings, to cut down on heating and air conditioning needs. The use of electricity to heat buildings and to heat water must be stopped. Electricity billing rates must be reformed. (At present the rates are written so that as use increases, the cost decreases. Thus large users benefit. To encourage cutbacks, the reverse must be established: rates must rise with increased electricity use.) Electric appliances need to be rated for their efficient use of electricity and the sale of wasteful ones banned. The emphasis of suggestions like these was to reduce energy demands and cut down on use.

Environmentalists generally supported the idea of cutting back. This would reduce the need for more energy production, which would help protect the environment. For this philosophy environmentalists became the subject of much criticism. Their ideas were labeled foolish, and they were blamed for helping to produce the energy crisis. After all, it was charged, their criticism had held up nuclear power plant construction, closed the large Santa Barbara coastal oil fields to new drilling, and prevented public utilities from using coal and some types of oil in generating electricity. Their actions had restricted the availability of energy even before the Arab oil embargo.

Energy Problem Studied

Several different studies of the energy problem had been made in 1972 and 1973. Two are of importance. One was made at the request of a committee of the California Legislature—the California Assembly Committee on Planning and Land Use. It had asked the Rand Corporation to study the energy situation and make recommendations. The second report was made by the Stanford Research Institute (SRI) at the request of five public utilities. The conflict between these two studies reflects the dispute between conservation-minded groups in California and the public utilities and industry.

The whole thrust of the SRI report was directed at how to meet energy needs. It was against setting limits on the use of electricity, which it said would upset the state's economy and increase the crisis. It also was opposed to raising rates to curtail consumption; prices should rise only to pay for increased electricity production, not to cut down use. The report also recommended a rapid increase of power generation from nuclear power plants.

In contrast, the Rand report showed a much greater interest in conserving energy and holding down demand until better ways can be found to produce power. The Rand study was not enthusiastic about nuclear power production. It was much more concerned with the environmental impact of energy use and production. Rand analysts did not believe that technology was going to solve energy production problems quickly, and they felt the task was to slow down demand, not to build a whole series of new power plants.

It is important to remember that the Rand study was prepared for a legislative committee. The Committee on Planning and Land Use, which asked for the report, directed that it be presented to one of its subcommittees. This subcommittee concentrated on studying the need for energy planning and policy, and the specific problem of providing California with electricity. It not only used the Rand report in its work, but also drew up a long questionnaire that was sent to several public utilities, environmental groups, and government agencies. The purpose of the questionnaire was to gather both a response to the Rand suggestions and information on what the state's role should be in forming energy policy. The subcommittee also held hearings to collect additional information.

Legislature Moves to Solve Energy Problems.   When these activities were completed, the chairman of the subcommittee, Assemblyman Charles Warren, announced a proposed solution to the energy crisis. He suggested the establishment of a five-member State Energy Resources Conservation and Development Commission. It was to organize the planning to be done for California's future energy needs, and support research into various alternate solutions such as the use of solar energy and geothermal or underground steam energy. Furthermore, the approval of new power plants was to be under the supervision of this commission.

Legislative Defeat.   Despite the clear identification of energy problems and legislative suggestions of how to meet them, nothing was accomplished. Assemblyman Warren found his proposals blocked. To overcome opposition and delaying measures within the Legislature, he joined with Senator Alfred Alquist to produce a compromise measure. The Warren–Alquist effort managed to win the Legislature's approval in the closing hours of the

1973 session. The heavy pressure against passage from the Public Utilities Commission, which feared reduction of its authority, from major private utility companies like Southern California Edison, Southern California Gas, and the Pacific Gas and Electric Company, and from the representative of the General Electric Company seemed to have failed. However, Governor Ronald Reagan soon vetoed the measure.

Warren–Alquist State Energy Resources Conservation and Development Act

The fuel crisis that hit California that winter brought renewed interest in energy solutions. The energy crisis was to have a priority position among legislative issues in 1974. Two proposals emerged. One was to create an energy czar who, with a panel of advisors, would make major decisions to deal with the situation. Speed limits, lighting needs, and the use of energy in general were to fall under his control. As the energy crisis lessened in the spring, the proposal was dropped. Major objections had surfaced to giving any one person such broad powers. The other suggestion, which did survive, was Assemblyman Warren's proposal from the previous year, which he and Senator Alquist pushed for adoption. This time the Reagan administration wished to negotiate. The result was a piece of compromise legislation that did pass the Legislature and was signed by the Governor in May 1974. It took effect in January of 1975. The General Electric representative intensely opposed it to the end, as did the American Home Appliance Manufacturers Association.

The Warren–Alquist Act clearly sets forth the state's policy on energy conservation and development. It establishes "the state's responsibility for energy resources," which includes "encouraging, developing, and coordinating research and development into energy supply and demand problems." And that involves the regulation of electrical generating and transmitting facilities. The purpose is "to reduce wasteful, uneconomical, and unnecessary uses of energy." By thus influencing the use of electricity and "reducing the rate of growth of energy" use, the state's "environmental, public safety, and land use goals" will be preserved.

This legislation created a full-time, five-member commission to carry out the policy. Each member of the new State Energy Resources Conservation and Development Commission must be qualified in a different field and serve for five years. One member is to be qualified in engineering or physical sciences and familiar with energy supply or conversion systems; another an attorney qualified in administrative law; another experienced in the field of environmental protection or the study of ecosystems; another an economist with experience in natural resource management, and the fifth member chosen from the general public.

This commission controls the use and development of all existing and potential energy sources. That includes the ability to limit energy use in brownouts and to restrict new service connections by electric utilities. Also, it certifies all new power plant sites and approves new sites even if local agencies object. This provision was most controversial, for the commission was to have the final say on such questions unless the Coastline Commissions were involved or the federal Atomic Energy Commission needed to approve the plan. Another controversial aspect of the law was the commission's power to set energy use standards for home appliances. Even though this represented a remarkable effort to eliminate the wasteful use of energy by some appliances, it aroused strong opposition, especially from national appliance manufacturers and the American Home Appliance Manufacturers Association. Lastly, the Warren–Alquist Act provides that state electrical users shall pay a small extra charge for the electricity they use, in order to finance research and development work in the energy field.

The creation of a powerful, independent commission was a very controversial feature of the 1973–74 Legislature. Yet it revealed the Legislature working carefully to develop machinery to come to grips with the energy crisis and, hopefully, prevent future energy shortages.[9]

Minorities in California Politics

We have been discussing the rising concern for the quality of the environment that has characterized the last few years. Another strong current has been a growing concern for the quality of life of minority groups. Since World War II, minority groups have increasingly attempted to be heard politically.

The Drive To Be Heard

The drive of the Third World to be heard has been felt in various events: the boycott on non-union table grapes and lettuce by the United Farm Workers; the Brown Berets' confrontation with the Los Angeles Board of Education; the Los Angeles (Watts) riots in 1965; the rise of the Black Panthers for Self-Defense in Oakland; Bobby Seale's 1973 campaign for mayor of Oakland; Thomas Bradley's 1973 election as mayor of Los Angeles; Wilson Riles' election as California's Superintendent of Public Instruction; the work of MAPA (the Mexican-American Political Association) and La Raza Unida; the Indian occupation of Alcatraz. To organize, to be heard, to demand change, to lead, to recognize themselves as a valid political group—these were some of the political goals that minority group organizers sought in the late 1960s. The problem has been, though, that for some strange, unexplained reason Anglos seemed to expect to hear a single voice from each group. What they heard, of course, was what they heard from their own group—a series of competing, conflicting voices. It is evident that divisions, as natural as they are, have all too often reduced the groups' political clout.

In the 1960s ethnic politics stressed civil rights, desegregation, and an end to discrimination. The focus was on distinct action through separate parties (such as La Raza Unida), separate groups, separate politics to achieve their goals. But seldom was that separateness successful on the political scene. For example, Chicano voters who registered under the unofficial La Raza Unida Party label, not as Democrats or Republicans, found themselves unable to vote in primaries.

Minority Groups and the Political Process

In the 1970s the same problems continue, but the growing emphasis of minority groups is on participation within the traditional political process to achieve their goals. That means increasing voter registration, participation on boards, committees and councils, and involvement in the traditional parties. While the goal of separateness has not been abandoned and ultimately may be achieved, for the moment greater participation is the most appropriate way to attain immediate success and to gain power in the political setting.[10]

Bobby Seale's Campaign.   An example of this change of direction was the campaign of Black Panther Party cofounder Bobby Seale for mayor of Oakland. Seale and Huey P. Newton founded the Black Panther Party in Oakland in 1966. Black Panthers have at times struggled violently with police in Oakland and elsewhere as well. Armed Panthers once even made a surprise visit to the floor of the California Assembly at the Capitol. Thus, to have Seale involved in a legitimate political campaign startled many Californians, who believed him to be a gun-waving fanatic. Yet the calm, carefully run campaign indicated that something new was happening. The issues were unemployment and crime—not confrontation and violence, as some may have feared or hoped.

A voter registration drive (35,000 were claimed to have been registered) and strong appeals to all minority groups were made to enlist members of the previously uninvolved minority population. Over half of Oakland's population is made up of Blacks and Chicanos, and Seale tried to capture that vote. The campaign centered on the difference in approach to the city's problems between the incumbent mayor and Seale. Seale stressed the need for consumer protection, safe streets, taxing stocks and bonds, and instituting a capital gains tax on corporations, whereas the mayor stressed the interests of business and the economy of the area. In the voting of May 1973, the mayor won reelection, but Seale received nearly 44,000 votes (36% of the vote). During the election, Seale's supporters distributed campaign literature to encourage a turnout and provided voters with transportation to the polls. His approach and appeal were broader and more traditional than most people had anticipated.

Seale refused to accept his defeat as final, saying he would stay in politics both to run again and to be active in supporting other candidates. The Panthers announced their intention of working on an initiative campaign for new local ordinances to achieve the objectives Seale had been discussing. The whole emphasis was on controlling city government and funneling city funds and energies into programs to benefit the community at large—and for Oakland that meant doing something for the poor and for minorities.[11]

Thomas Bradley's Election.   Much more successful than Seale's campaign was that of Los Angeles City Councilman Thomas Bradley for mayor of Los Angeles. He ran against Samuel Yorty, who was seeking reelection for a fourth term, in a strongly waged, sometimes bitter campaign. Two major underlying issues were Bradley's color and Yorty's length of time in office. Yorty had been mayor for 12 years, and during that time, Bradley charged, had displayed a lack of leadership and a tendency to play favorites and take care of special interests. Yorty, on the other hand, charged that well-hidden radicals were secretly planning Bradley's campaign, and that Bradley's position on law enforcement was weak. The undertone of such charges, as Bradley's being antipolice, was Bradley's color. Racism surfaced on various occasions during the campaign, both in Yorty's own remarks and in his campaign advertising.

Los Angeles voters, however, apparently agreed with much of Bradley's criticism. Bradley was elected mayor in May 1973 by a rather wide margin. He has proved to be a very activist mayor, revitalizing the mayor's position within Los Angeles city government by vigorously attacking serious problems facing the city. He represents the trend of minority group members who participate actively within the political process, and he has emerged as a major figure within the Democratic Party.

Ruben Ayala's Election.   Another example of this effort to expand participation in the government process was the unexpected election in January 1974 of Ruben S. Ayala to the California Senate. In a district in which it seemed impossible to win, Ayala ran a successful campaign, using the atmosphere of Watergate scandals and the energy crisis as his major issues. Running against a Republican Assemblyman in a traditionally conservative area, Democrat Ayala's victory was indeed startling. He became the first Mexican since 1911 to sit in the very traditionally oriented State Senate. In the November 1974 general election Ayala was elected to a full term in the Senate. At that same election a second Mexican American Assemblyman Alex García was elected to the Senate.

Dymally and Fong Election.   The gains of minority candidates grew on the statewide level in the November 1974 general election. Joining Wilson Riles (reelected in June 1974 as Superintendent) to hold statewide office were Mervyn Dymally and March Fong. Fong, a Chinese American, was elected Secretary of State. Trinidad-born Dymally became the first Black to win the Lieutenant Governorship. The election of Fong (a former member of the Assembly) and Dymally (a former State Senator) well illustrates the continuing and growing pattern of political participation of minority group members.

School Integration Problems

Beyond this shift in methods, a change occurred in the drive for integration. Integration becomes especially controversial when shifting school boundaries and busing are suggested as a means of bringing together various groups for a common rather than a separate education, so that they may better learn to understand and appreciate one another. Results have not always been favorable. Busing for whatever reason can be a nightmare of scheduling and transportation problems. In addition, when moves to integrate were made, minority parents discovered that their children were usually the ones bused. Also, their children were often ignored—at times personally but more often culturally—in the newly integrated schools. Integration for many thus meant an attack on their cultural heritage. To change this, programs and textbooks were written to include new material to correct obvious slights. But still the result was not always a success. Some people felt that perhaps separate schools, each with quality education, were actually the best way to prevent the destruction of distinct cultural heritages. An excellent example of this controversy occurred recently in Sacramento.

In response to earthquake dangers, school districts in California were required to repair buildings to bring them up to state earthquake safety standards, or abandon them. Sacramento counted 13 inner-city schools that did not meet those standards. They happened to be older schools in the central part of the city, schools attended by large groups of minority students. Thus, the question of integration became one aspect of the problem of building replacement. Several choices were available to the school board: rebuild the schools, replace them, rebuild only a few, or bus all or some of the children elsewhere. Opposition began to develop to anything but reconstructing or replacing some of the central city schools, which would result in segregated schools. Some Black, Chicano, and Asian community individuals spoke strongly in favor of ethnic schools. They formed the ABC (Asians, Blacks, Chicanos) Committee to support the maintenance of neighborhood schools that would reflect the community around them, and preserve the cultural integrity and heritage of each community. Furthermore, they wanted minority personnel attached to neighborhood schools to reinforce the total ethnic concept.

The overriding concern was not integration or segregation but cultural heritage. The issue became one of whether integrated or segregated schools would best serve to protect the diverse cultural heritages existing in the central city. Opposition then developed quickly to the segregated ethnic school, and the school board and school administration were caught between the factions of the ethnic community. The National Association for the Advancement of Colored People objected strongly to the segregation idea and threatened to sue if it were implemented. The County Attorney's office ruled that the school district had to have racially integrated schools.

The issue truly present was the need, the desirability, the value of separateness. The relationship of school quality to integration was being questioned and debated. That was remarkable considering the great drive launched for integrated schools and the broad acceptance of that goal in the 1950s and 1960s. At that time integrated schools were thought to be a major advance for ethnic groups. The 1970s found that entire premise being questioned. Of course, this issue is not unique to Sacramento. San Francisco's Chinese residents in Chinatown—the largest Chinese community in the country—objected strongly to integrated schools, fearing that such an educational setup would destroy their vital cultural background.

Ethnic Groups Emphasize Specific Goals

For the 1970s it appeared that ethnic politics would select some specific goals to emphasize. Greater stress was placed on preserving the cultural heritage of a group, even if segregation were required to do so. More stress also was placed on minority individuals' moving onto boards, committees, and commissions in an effort to influence those government elements directly affecting the quality of life of the community.

Aiding that drive was the effort of city, county, and state bodies to include more minority representation. In 1973, for instance, the Los Angeles County Board of Supervisors required monthly reports from county department heads on the ethnic backgrounds of county employees. The

Supervisors wanted to know the difference between an ethnic group's percentage of the county's work force and its percentage of the county's population. State departments such as the Department of Education announced their intention to promote ethnic minorities and women whenever possible, to achieve greater balance within their work forces.

Surveys showed that very little change was taking place, however. The Sacramento *Bee* in January 1973 published a survey of Sacramento City and County commissions and found that appointments usually went to white males over 30 (see Figure 5). This type of survey suggests that if minorities do wish to join boards and commissions, it will be a challenging and frustrating process. Still, if the drive to participate in this fashion grows, the political process may welcome it in preference to the confrontation and extreme pressure tactics previously popular. Chicano and Black politics seem headed in the direction of participation, moving away from separate identification for the moment in order to achieve immediate goals. Bobby Seale, for example, continually identified himself in the Oakland campaign as a Democrat. Separatist parties and groups will remain, but they will probably be secondary to a greater effort to become involved in the more traditional government and party system.

Federal Funds

To solve many of the problems of the 1970s money was going to be needed and in great quantity. Air and water quality standards simply cannot be met without spending money to control and stop pollution at its source. For some items, such as antipollution devices for cars, the cost must be assumed by the owner. But for others, local and state governments must spend the money. High water quality, for instance, will require more elaborate and more efficient sewage disposal plants, some costing millions of dollars. In some instances federal funds are available. For the Sacramento problem discussed earlier, the federal government will provide 75 percent of the funds if the state and local government will each put up 12½ percent. Because the project may cost $240 million, outside aid both for the local government and the state becomes very important.

The Effect of Federal Funds in the West

It is traditional and fashionable for Westerners to mention and take pride in their independence. Indeed, at times it appears that the West literally financed and built itself without outside help—especially from easterners and from the federal government. It is quite true that eastern private investment in the West usually has been low, yet easterners did invest in and help to build the West—through their federal taxes. Thus, while

	Authorized Strength	No. Appointed by City & County	City: Appointed by City	City: Male	City: Female	City: Over 30	City: Under 30	City: White	City: Black	City: Asian	City: Mexican	County: Appointed by County	County: Male	County: Female	County: Over 30	County: Under 30	County: White	County: Black	County: Asian	County: Mexican	Vacancies to be filled by City & County
Air Pollution Control Hearing Board	5	3										3	3		3		2	1			2
Assessment Appeals Boards (incl. two alternates)	8	8										8	7	1	8		8				
City Civil Service Board	5	5	5	5		5		2	1	1	1										
County Civil Service Commission	5	5										5	5		5		4			1	
Community Center Authority	5	5	3	3		3		3				2	2		2		2				
Golden Empire Regional Comprehensive Health Council	43	17										17	13	4	16	1	13	2	2		1
Government Reorganization Committee	40	37	17	13½*	3½	17		13	1½	1	1½	20	16½	3½	20		19	½		½	3
Housing Authority	7	7	3½	3½		3½		2½	1			3½	2½	1	3½		3½				
Human Relations Commission	12**	11	6	4	2	5	1	3	1	1	1	5	3	2	5		2	2		1	1
Local Agency Formation Commission	5	1***										1	1		1		1				
Sacramento-Yolo Mosquito Abatement District	9	2	1	1		1		1				1	1		1		1				
City Planning Commission	9	9	9	8	1	9		7		2											
County Planning Commission	5	5										5	5		5		5				
Sacramento-Yolo Port District	5	4	2	2		2		2				2	2		2		2				
County Recreation and Park Commission	5	5										5	5		5		5				
Redevelopment Agency	7	7	7	6	1	7		7													
Regional Transit District	7	7	4	4		4		3	1			3	3		2	1	3				
SAEOC (Sacramento Area Economic Opportunity Coun.)	24	1	1	1		1		1													1
Sacramento Transit Authority	7	5***	5	5		5		4	1												
Zoning Board of Adjustment (incl. one alternate)	3	3										3	2	1	3		3				
Totals		147	63½	56	7½	62½	1	48½	6½	5	3½	83½	71	12½	81½	2	73½	5½	2	2½	8
Percentage				88.9	11.1	98.5	1.5	76.4	10.2	7.9	5.5		85.0	15.0	97.6	2.4	88.0	6.6	2.4	2.9	

* Use of ½ indicates appointment shared by City and County
** In addition, three members appointed by the Sacramento Youth Council are under 21 years of age
*** Excludes persons who serve by reason of other office, such as County Supervisors

Figure 5. Race, Sex, Age Balance on Civic Appointments

private investment built the East, public federal funds were invested to build western states. In fact, it has not been unusual for federal expenditures in the West to be greater than the amount of federal taxes collected from the western states. Money has been spent on freeways and highway building in general, on reclamation programs such as the large Central Valley Project, on waterways to provide flood control and to improve water transportation, in the aerospace and defense industry for military bases, and much more.

In 1930, federal funds spent in California totaled $130 million, by 1945 $8.5 billion. Many Californians and westerners refused to acknowledge the federal government's huge commitment to developing and sustaining major projects in the West. By 1973, however, the measure of that spending became a painful reality. By that time the Nixon administration had begun cutting back on federal spending and impounding congressionally allocated money, thus leaving more and more programs to the state for funding. It was estimated that nearly $2 billion of federal money would be lost to California that year because of Nixon budget cuts in the prime areas of education support, and agricultural, environmental, and water resource programs. Despite these reductions California still stood to receive up to $30 billion from the federal government in 1973, about 11 percent of all federal spending. The 1974 federal budget raised the amount of California's share of federal funds to $33 billion, still about 11 percent of the budget. Thus, despite federal cuts, federal investment continued at a high level in California, and it is expected to be of major importance in helping to solve the problems of the 1970s.[12]

Tax Reform

The reduction in federal spending in California has helped to focus attention on state spending and taxation. As the federal government has withdrawn its aid in some areas, the question has been how California could compensate for the cuts. This, of course, has raised the entire issue of ever-increasing state spending and the need for tax reform.

Nearly everyone subscribes to the need for tax reform. Yet few substantial tax changes were made by 1975. A major effort had been launched to reform school financing, but in itself, this was not terribly far-reaching or adequate, a point to be discussed later in greater detail.

Reagan's Proposition 1

In 1973, Governor Ronald Reagan launched an intensive campaign to secure voter approval of a revenue control and tax reduction program. His proposal was an initiative constitutional amendment presented to Californians as Proposition 1 in a November 1973 special election. Gener-

ally, the initiative proposed to set a constitutional limit on taxes, to provide
a continuing year-by-year reduction of income taxes, to require a two-thirds
vote in the Legislature to change tax legislation, to place a maximum
ceiling on local property tax rates, and to force the state to pay for any
new services required of local governments.

Reagan's proposal met with heavy criticism. The issues raised by the
initiative were complicated and almost defied careful explanation and
understanding. However, a basic question raised was who should determine
tax policy, and whether or not a firm constitutional tax lid was really
the way to bring economy to state government. The integrity of the
Legislature to do its job in setting tax policy was at issue; the amendment
would have restricted its ability to provide for state needs. In the end,
California voters firmly rejected Reagan's ideas, but despite that rejection
the initiative had succeeded in focusing attention on the need for a review
of state spending and state taxing policies. Real tax reform was needed.[13]

Other Tax Reform Proposals

Several specific suggestions emerged following the defeat of Reagan's tax
scheme. One was to reform the state income tax by tying to it a cost-of-
living element. Ordinarily, as a person's income rises, he moves to a new,
higher tax bracket. At the same time, he finds inflation has eaten up his
increased spending power. Income taxes do not take into account that
an increased income does not always mean expanded purchasing power.
This proposal calls for adjustments in the tax brackets to take into account
inflation. The tax would increase only as actual spending power increased.

Another recommendation was to do away with property taxes on
most single-family homes occupied by their owners. The reasoning behind
this was that because this property is not income-producing it should not
be taxed. Another proposal advocated that farm land and open space areas
be removed from property taxation, if the owner promises to retain the
property as such.

Other proposals suggest eliminating the sales tax on items such as
soap and razors, and on clothing except for more expensive articles. Such
reforms, along with the property tax ideas outlined above, would benefit
lower- and middle-income groups, but ways would have to be found to
make up the lost revenues. For this, an expanded income tax has been
suggested. The increased income tax would hit those in lower-income levels
far less harshly than the present system does, but in total it would provide
the necessary new tax income.

The 1974 Legislature did carefully consider one tax reform. It was
a constitutional amendment that would make it easier to raise the taxes
on banks, corporations, and insurance companies. Sales and income taxes
can be raised by a simple majority vote of the Legislature, but a two-thirds

vote is required to increase business taxes. By its terms, business taxes also could be raised by a simple majority vote of the Legislature. Because the Constitution established the two-thirds vote requirement, an amendment had to be presented to the voters for their approval. Reformers thought the voters would approve, because many feel business does not carry its fair share of taxation. The Legislature, however, failed to approve the amendment for the November 1974 ballot.

It is apparent that even though tax reform has been a steadily discussed topic, major reform will be difficult to secure because of the complexity of the issues and the opposition of the interests who benefit from the current system.

Financing Public Education

Serrano v. Priest Decision

One of the basic causes of rising tax rates has been the task of financing public education. In 1971, in a decision known as *Serrano* v. *Priest*, the California Supreme Court ruled that the method of school financing as it then stood was unconstitutional, primarily because it discriminated against the poorer districts in the state. The court's ruling attacked the principle of using only local property taxes to support local schools. The problem was that for some districts in poor areas, even high property tax rates did not raise enough money. Other districts were rich and so even a low tax rate raised quite a bit of money.° A child's education then varied from district to district because of the amount of money each district was able to invest in education. Education was therefore unequal because of the method of funding, so the Court ruled against school districts' continuing to use that means of school financing. In 1972, as a result of the decision, the Legislature passed a measure providing for a vast increase in state aid to school districts. The state's share of school costs

---

°This may seem difficult to understand, so let's look at an example. Suppose School District A and School District B each have 500 homes. The tax rate in District A is $1.00 per $100 of value of each house, and the average house in the district is worth $20,000, so the average homeowner pays about $200 in taxes, and the district receives $100,000 in revenue ($200 x 500 taxpayers).

In District B, the tax rate is $.50 per $100 of value of each house, but the average home in the district is worth $175,000, so the average homeowner pays about $875 in taxes, and the district receives $437,500 in revenue ($875 x 500 taxpayers).

Let's say that there are 500 children in each district. District A will be able to spend $200 on each child's education. District B will be able to spend $875 per child, even though the tax rate is only half as much as the rate in District A.

This is a greatly simplified example, but it will give you some idea of how the system works, when only local property taxes are used to finance the schools in the district.

rose substantially as a result of the measure. It soon became apparent, though, that the new law did not really begin to level out the spending between rich and poor districts; it was filled with loopholes and rather odd provisions. For instance, the richer districts under this law were actually encouraged to raise their tax rates, thus giving them increasingly more money to spend on their students than those in poorer districts. Equality remained to be achieved.

Thus, the search continued for a more equitable way to fund public schools. The effect of the original *Serrano* v. *Priest* decision broadened in 1974. Originally, the case had begun in 1968 in Los Angeles Superior Court. The first judge to hear the case dismissed it. At that time, though, an appeal was made to the California Supreme Court. That court in 1971 said an issue did indeed exist for proper court consideration. Then the Supreme Court returned the case to the Los Angeles Superior Court for further deliberations on other questions of school financing and the relationship between that financing and the quality of the schools.

New Decision 1974

In May of 1974, the Superior Court finished its examination of those issues involved and stated its findings. It found that under California's State Constitution, not only the original method of school financing, but also the 1972 legislative effort at reform was unconstitutional. The judge of this court pointed out that no constitutional provisions ordered a particular quality of education. But the Constitution did demand that whatever education was offered to California children had to be equal. Because present school financing methods provided unequal funding, equal education was not assured. The funding provided by the 1972 reform effort was as unequal as the former system had been. Even though this Superior Court decision was to be appealed, most people believed the California Supreme Court would confirm it.

Almost immediately, therefore, great discussion and speculation developed over what kind of school financing the courts would accept as constitutional. Several suggestions were made in the 1974 Superior Court ruling, others were being put together within the Department of Education, and still others were being studied by both Senate and Assembly Education committees of the Legislature. Because the case was still to be reviewed by the Supreme Court and because 1974 was an election year, no one really wanted to engage in a serious effort to shift taxes or to discuss new taxes. Not until 1975 was legislation going to be actively pursued to handle the latest effects of the *Serrano* v. *Priest* case.

Suggested Solutions

Despite this situation several solutions were proposed. The most obvious was a call for 100 percent state funding of California schools. This would do away with the local school property tax. To raise the necessary money, a statewide property tax was suggested. This was within court guidelines. As a state tax, it would be applied equally throughout California. The state would gather the income and distribute it on an equal per pupil basis. Areas contributing high tax income were to contribute their excess to areas bringing in very low amounts of tax money, resulting in equal financing of all districts.

A similar proposal called for doing away with any school property tax and raising sales and income taxes to provide money for full state funding. One major objection to any 100 percent state funding proposal was that such a system might weaken or destroy local control over schools.

Another suggestion was to redraw school district boundaries completely. The purpose here was to form fewer districts which would have about equal tax bases for their revenue. This would provide equal funding and the new, larger districts would retain local control.

Power equalizing or equalization was an additional scheme under review. This concept would be an addition to the present financing setup instead of a replacement. In power equalizing the state would force wealthier tax-producing areas to share their tax money with the poorer tax base areas in the state.

The importance of the 1974 Superior Court decision was that it required the Legislature to come to grips with the problem of equalizing educational funding. A school district's income could no longer be tied to its property wealth, a situation that had produced great inequality. Because 1972 legislative action to reform financing had failed, newer ideas had to be studied. School financing would remain a serious problem throughout the 1970s.

One major threat, of course, was that the courts might take action if state government did not. The courts had been forced to order a solution to the legislative reapportionment problem when the Governor and Legislature could not agree on proper redistricting. Would the court act similarly on school financing if no acceptable solutions were forthcoming? To avoid that and to sidestep the entire issue, it was seriously suggested that California's Constitution be amended to make the current financing structure constitutional. That would legalize and freeze current practices no matter how unequal. But it would avoid the difficulty of having to handle the entire problem.[14]

A Series of Challenges

California government in the 1970s faces a series of major challenges, among them broad environmental issues, transportation problems, tax issues, and ethnic groups' effort to participate in the political process. The only element present in all of them is that of change—a change of attitude towards water projects, freeways, and the tactics of ethnic politics. The task of state government is to accept this world of issues, and working from the basis of continuing change, find solutions.

Review Questions

Air Pollution

What is air pollution and what are some of its effects on our lives?

How widespread is air pollution?

Who is in charge of air pollution control?

What solutions have been proposed to reduce air pollution?

Transportation Needs

What does *multimodal* mean?

What one mode of transportation has been used traditionally in California?

What modes are being considered now, and why?

What are the basic goals of the Department of Transportation?

Land Use Problems

Why are Californians more concerned than ever before, over the proper use of land?

What is the Environmental Quality Act? What does it require?

What was the Friends of Mammoth lawsuit?

What is "open space"? What is the work of the BCDC?

What does the California Coastal Zone Conservation Act call for? What is the significance of this act?

Water Needs

What is the purpose of the California Water Project?

What are the controversial features of the Project?

Why has resistance developed to the Project?

What are the key features of the Porter–Cologne Water Quality Control Act? What has been the criticism of the Porter–Cologne Act?

What is the State Water Resources Control Board?

Energy Crisis

What is the problem?

Why are environmentalists so concerned about it?

What is the public utilities' view of the energy crisis?

What solutions have been proposed?

Which branch of government moved to solve the crisis?

What energy legislation was passed in 1974?

What is the State Energy Resources Conservation and Development Commission and what are its responsibilities?

Ethnic and Minority Groups

What are some current political goals of minority groups?

Have those goals been met? If not, why not?

Why has the goal of more minority participation in the traditional political process become important?

How has the goal of racial integration changed in the minds of some minority members?

Federal Funding

How have federal funds aided western development?

How do federal cutbacks hinder California?

Tax Reform

Who made the Revenue Control and Tax Reduction proposal?

What were its key features?

What other tax reform proposals have been made?

Financing Public Education

What was the *Serrano* v. *Priest* decision?

What solutions have been proposed to the problem identified in *Serrano* v. *Priest?*

Notes

1. Bob Simmons, "State Lags in Clearing the Air," *California Journal* 4 (October, 1973): 330–332.

2. Ed Salzman, "The Decline (and Fall?) of the Highway Empire," *California Journal* 4 (September, 1973): 305–306.

3. Harre W. Demoro, "What BART Can Teach Los Angeles," *California Journal* 4 (October, 1973): 325–329.

4. "Recent Supreme Court Decisions," *California Journal* 3 (October, 1972): 316.

5. "Coastline Commissions—What Have They Done? An Interview with Joseph Bodovitz, Executive Director," *California Journal* 4 (November, 1973): 377–379.

6. Jud Clark and Lance Olson, "1974 Legislature: Who Controls the Land?" *California Journal* 4 (November, 1973): 380–384. See also William Lipman, "Can States Live with Congress' Land-Use Bills?" *California Journal* 4 (November, 1973): 384.

7. Tom Harris, "Finding Water to Keep California Green," *California Journal* 4 (October, 1973): 345–347.

8. "The Fight Against Water Pollution—a Sellout or a Realistic Attack on One of California's Toughest Problems?" *California Journal* 3 (February, 1972): 52–55.

9. The *California Journal* devoted almost an entire issue to an excellent discussion of the developing energy crisis. See the June, 1973, issue; Maureen Fitzgerald, "What Does What in the Energy Crisis," *California Journal* 4 (December, 1973): 407–409; Robert J. Markson, "The Economics of the Energy Crisis," *California Journal* 4 (December, 1973): 410–411; "How the New Energy Act Should Work," *California Journal* 5 (July, 1974): 239–240.

10. Juan Manuel Herrera, " 'Years of Shout' Seem over in Chicano Politics," *California Journal* 4 (May, 1973): 155–158. See also Suzanne Barba, "The Awakening of Another Political Giant," *California Journal* 5 (October, 1974): 344–345.

11. Robert Feinbaum, "How the Whites Keep Control of Oakland," *California Journal* 4 (December, 1973): 419–420.

12. Nash, *The American West*, pp. 202, 233–240. Gerald Nash has a very enlightening discussion of the tremendous impact federal funds have had on California and Western history.

13. Jerome Evans, "Governor Reagan Proposes Constitutional Amendment to Place a Ceiling on State's Revenues," *California Journal* 4 (March, 1973): 80–82; "Reagan Explains His Tax-Limit Plan in an Interview," *California Journal* 4 (April, 1973): 132–133; "Special Section: The Reagan Tax Initiative," *California Journal* 4 (September, 1973); Bruce Keppel, "Proposition One: Who's Playing Politics with the Tax Limit?" *California Journal* 4 (October, 1973): 339–341; Bruce Keppel, "An Offer Californians Did Refuse," *California Journal* 4 (December, 1973): 400–403.

14. "Statewide Property Tax for Schools," *California Journal* 2 (March, 1971): 72–73, 85; "Large Urban School Districts—the Potential Victims of *Serrano*," *California Journal* 5 (May, 1974): 169–170; Minot W. Tripp,

"An Easy Way Out of *Serrano*—Legalizing the Status Quo," *California Journal* 5 (June, 1974): 203–204; Ronald A. Zumbrum and John H. Findley, "Yet Another View of *Serrano*," *California Journal* 5 (August, 1974): 279; Ronald Blubough, "A Philosophical Struggle within the Supreme Court," *California Journal* 5 (November, 1974): 382–384.

CHAPTER THREE

THE CONSTITUTIONAL SETTING AND POLITICAL REFORM

Overview

This section discusses the original structure of California government and recent efforts to reform that structure and its operation. In addition, it describes the constitutional provisions that provide for citizen participation in government. This includes a look at how constitutional amendments are proposed, the use of the direct legislation process of initiative and referendum, recall, election scheduling, and current voter qualifications.

The chapter also reviews efforts to reform the political process. Ballot pamphlet preparation, campaign spending limits and reports, financial disclosures, conflicts of interest, and lobbying are discussed. You should pay particular attention to the material on conflicts of interest and lobbying—both will be discussed in later chapters.

The California Constitution

The present government structure designed to meet the needs of California was first established in 1849. Its form represented a remarkable departure from Spanish and Mexican administrative efforts. In 1879, this constitution was greatly revised; it was accepted by voters in May of that year, and has remained in effect to the present.

State versus Federal Constitutions

From time to time a question arises as to which is dominant—the California or the United States Constitution. The United States Supreme Court does not rule on issues in which federal rights are not involved, or when a particular case focuses on state law. This has been an important point. In certain cases the California Supreme Court has based its decision on

California constitutional provisions. Thus, when similar cases were reviewed by the federal court and different rulings made, these findings
did not affect the validity of the California decisions. One such case was
the previously discussed *Serrano* v. *Priest,* which has continued to have
a profound influence on school financing.[1]

A Constitution and a Code of Law

The 1879 Constitution proved to have quite a different tone from the
1849 version. The group that wrote the second constitution happened
to be drawn from several very vocal, influential groups of the period.
They were able to make certain that their special interests and needs
were taken care of. Consequently, the 1879 Constitution was longer than
the first one, and quite importantly, its writing introduced the practice
of adding sections to handle very specific needs. Ordinarily, these detailed
sections would be part of a state's legal codes, but the early practice
set the pattern. From then on, sections to aid special state interest groups
would be written into the Constitution. Thus, the major drawback of this
1879 Constitution was that it did more than establish the general government structure, establish boundaries on state authority, or set forth basic
constitutional concepts—it included legislation. By 1973, some 662 amendments had been proposed and 388 adopted. (All but a few were offered
to voters by the Legislature.) The Constitution became more and more
a code of law rather than a constitution. The result was a lengthy document
badly in need of revision.

But the problem was how to accomplish that, because the Constitution
allowed only one process—constitutional conventions—to deal with large-
scale reform. Finally, in 1962, the Legislature gave California voters the
opportunity to approve an easier way to update their Constitution by
complete or partial changes. The voters agreed to the idea, and in 1963
the Legislature acted to establish a Constitutional Revision Commission.
The work began.

Constitutional Revision Commission

Why was reform needed? Outdated, conflicting, and confusing material
needed to be removed (a provision dealing with dueling, for instance).
The length needed to be cut, because so many amendments had been
added the Constitution had increased from 16,000 to 80,000 words—the
fourth longest document of its type in the world. The revision was to
stress retaining the basic government structure, the basic duties and responsibilities of government, and the fundamental rights of the people, while
removing much unnecessary language.

The Process

To accomplish this reform, the Revision Commission was to determine the problem sections and recommend changes to the Legislature. The Legislature was to act on these changes and place the resulting recommendations before the people as constitutional amendments. The Commission, first appointed in 1963, eventually included 60 citizen members and 20 legislators. Its work began in early 1964. Its procedure was to study the Constitution on an article by article basis. Meeting monthly, it considered specific articles and necessary changes. A committee of the Commission usually made recommendations based on background studies prepared by the Commission staff or suggested by outside consultants. Many hours went into preparing background studies, holding committee meetings to draw up recommendations, and conducting commission hearings in which final recommendations were heard.

The Results

The first results were presented to the Legislature in February 1966. That November, the first sweeping revisions were accepted by the voters. Especially significant were basic changes made in the Legislature's operations. Later recommendations, such as the educational and tax reforms, were not adopted by the Legislature. In addition, voters were much more selective in approving suggestions as time went on.

In 1971, the Commission finished its work and sent its final recommended revisions to the Legislature. By this time many of the suggestions of the Commission had been accepted by California voters. Over 31,000 words had been eliminated from the Constitution, and a more workable document had emerged.

Revision, though, needed to be continued. Constitutional revision did remain the goal of one group—the League of Women Voters. The League worked actively to convince legislators of the need to continue simplifying and better organizing the Constitution. They had some success in getting the Legislature to present more revision proposals to the voters.[2]

Direct Legislation

The Constitution's excessive length was in part the result of frequent amending by California voters. Amendments had been necessary because the original document was too long and too detailed. Several amendment procedures are allowed. For example, if a two-thirds vote is obtained, the Legislature may propose amendments or revisions to voters (the practice most often used), or it may ask permission to call a convention to prepare revisions. The state's voters also may propose changes directly, by use of the initiative process.

Figure 6.   Constitutional Amendments

- May be proposed by the initiative process, or the Legislature acting on a two-thirds vote.
- Become effective with a majority vote the day following the balloting.
- May be changed only by a vote of the electorate.

The Initiative

Californians can use the initiative procedure to propose their own laws and amendments. Proposals for laws or statutes are *initiative statutes*. Proposals for amendments are *initiative constitutional amendments*.

In order to qualify an initiative for the ballot, petitions must be circulated to obtain a required number of signatures. If the voters approve the initiative, it goes into effect. Initiative statutes require fewer signatures to qualify for the ballot than do amendments. This provision exists to encourage the greater use of initiative statutes over amendments. The reason is that amendments may be changed only by passing other amendments, whereas initiative statutes are more flexible, and some permit changes by the Legislature without requiring voter approval. In addition, initiative statutes do not become part of the Constitution and, therefore, do not lengthen it or burden it with unnecessary detail. Figure 7 explains the basic details of the initiative process.

The Referendum

Through the referendum, California voters can review almost any action of the Legislature. If citizens object to a law (or part of a law) that has been passed, they may circulate petitions, collecting signatures in order to propose its rejection in a referendum measure on the ballot. Figure 8 lists the important characteristics of the referendum procedure.

Examples of Initiatives

Direct legislation powers have been very important in bringing change to California government. The Coastal Zone Conservation Act was an initiative statute passed because the Legislature had failed to take action. Governor Reagan's suggestion about a tax ceiling is an example of the use of the initiative constitutional amendment procedure. Reagan used this method because the Legislature had failed to present a legislative constitutional amendment to the voters.

Figure 7.   The Initiative

What it does:

The initiative is the electorate's means of
- proposing statutes,
- proposing amendments to the Constitution, and
- adopting or rejecting those proposals.

How it gets on the ballot:
- Initiatives are proposed by presenting the Secretary of State with a petition stating the proposed statute or amendment.
- Petitions for *statutes* must include voter signatures in number equal to 5% of all votes cast for candidates for Governor in the last gubernatorial election.
- Petitions for *amendments* to the Constitution require signatures equal to 8% of the total vote for Governor in the last gubernatorial election.

The election:
- Initiatives are then presented to voters at either general or special elections.
- Approval requires a majority of votes; if approved, the measure becomes effective the day after the election.

How it can be changed:
- Initiative *statutes* may be changed or repealed by the Legislature only if it submits, by a majority vote, a new statute to the voters for their approval. (Some initiative statutes permit amendments or repeal without voter approval.)
- Initiative *amendments* may only be changed or repealed by the adoption of a new amendment. The amendment may be proposed by a new initiative, or by the Legislature's two-thirds vote proposing a new amendment.

Where it can be used:
- Initiative powers may be used by voters in cities and counties according to procedures established by the Legislature, or if local city and county charters provide for their use.

Figure 8.   The Referendum

What it does:
- The referendum is the electorate's power to approve or reject laws or parts of laws passed by the Legislature.

What it can not do:
The referendum cannot be used to reject
- An *urgency statute or law* (when an urgency section is approved by a two-thirds vote of the Senate and Assembly, it takes effect immediately).
- statutes calling elections,
- laws setting taxes, or
- laws establishing appropriations.

How it gets on the ballot:
- A referendum is proposed by presenting the Secretary of State with a petition which includes signatures equal to 5% of the total votes cast for Governor at the last gubernatorial election.
- A referendum petition must be presented on a given measure within 90 days after the Legislature passed it.

What is required to pass a referendum:
- Approval requires a majority of votes. The measure becomes effective the day following the election.

How it can be changed:
- The Legislature may change or repeal referendum laws.

Sometimes an initiative can produce interesting results. In 1933, voters amended the Constitution to provide that gasoline taxes in California could be used only for the construction, improvement, repairs, and maintenance of the state's highways. Recently, environmentalists have wanted to use a portion of this tax revenue for transportation modes other than highways. Not until June 1974 did voters approve the necessary amendment. On another occasion in 1947, voters changed social welfare provisions by an amendment that wrote in the names of three supporters who were to serve in state government and who were thus guaranteed jobs! Only a later vote in 1949 changed that and prevented it from happening again.

The initiative can hinder future flexibility in solving state problems. This is one reason why the 1973 Reagan tax proposal was so feared: it would have committed the state to a specific tax program by a constitutional amendment. If the proposal did not work, it could not be changed until voters repealed it!

A final point should be remembered. No initiative can be implemented if it violates the provisions of the California Constitution or the United States Constitution. In 1964, a very controversial initiative constitutional amendment known as Proposition 14 was approved by voters. It overturned California fair housing laws and in 1966, the California Supreme Court ruled that it violated provisions of the United States Constitution. The United States Supreme Court upheld this decision in 1967.

Circulating Petitions

A major problem of the initiative and referendum process for those groups who want to use it is the need to gather so many voter signatures on petitions. To collect a few hundred thousand signatures takes a great deal of work and some groups have hired professionals to complete the task. For example, Governor Reagan's effort to qualify his tax reduction proposal included paying professionals 30 cents a signature to obtain the proper number. This practice has greatly irritated some people, who have questioned the real motive behind an initiative, referendum, or recall if individuals must be paid to gather voter signatures. Real reform seems lost in this type of drive. Instead, it appears that well-to-do groups are using the process for their own benefit. This may mean that in a state as large as California only well-financed or well-organized groups with large memberships will have access to the constitutional machinery designed to bring change because only they can secure the necessary signatures or pay for securing them, fund the advertising campaign needed to awaken the voter to the issue, and motivate him to vote for it. While it does give voters direct access to the political system, direct legislation, for all its worth, has special drawbacks and can become a tool of special interests.

Voter Pamphlets

To help voters to understand ballot measures, the Secretary of State distributes a voters' pamphlet. For each measure (including bonds) the pamphlet sets forth the actual text of the proposal, analyzes it, and estimates its financial effect, and summarizes arguments for and against it.

Because ballot pamphlets have been noted traditionally for their unclear and obscure writing, a drive has been launched recently to improve them. One indication that change was needed came in 1972, when the Secretary of State's office discovered that arguments both for and against a specific proposition had been written by the same person. A pamphlet reform measure was passed by the 1973 legislature and the June 1974 primary marked the first effort to distribute better election materials to voters.

In that same June primary California voters approved a new initiative statute known as the Political Reform Act of 1974. Among the reforms approved was a section on ballot pamphlets. The minimum size of the pamphlet, the minimum size of type, the organization and layout, the requirements of the analysis for each measure, and a provision for art work were some of the items specifically detailed. Also, before future pamphlets are printed, they must be available for public review. If any voter believes the information to be incorrect, he may initiate court action to make it accurate. This measure was an important step in producing voters who are more fully informed about the state measures on which they vote.

Recall

Closely related to the idea of voter participation through direct legislation is recall, the voters' power to remove any elected public official from office. (Because United States Representatives and Senators are not state officials, they are not subject to recall.) Figure 9 summarizes some important points about recall procedures.

One of the more striking aspects of recall is that if the measure fails, the state must pay the election expenses of the official subjected to the proceeding. When a recall campaign was directed against Governor Reagan in 1968 some critics pointed out that if the effort failed, the state would have to pay all of Reagan's election expenses. In some circles, this fact substantially weakened the recall campaign, which never succeeded in qualifying for the ballot.

Elections

Once petitions for initiative, referendum, or recall have enough signatures to meet the minimum required, and after these petitions are examined and found to qualify, an election is held. Recall elections must be called within 80 days following qualification. Initiative and referendum elections are combined with the next general election, or the Governor may call a special election. Frequently, special elections are called to coincide with regularly scheduled elections, such as the direct primary, to cut costs. One controversy over Governor Reagan's tax proposal was that he called a special election for November 1973 rather than waiting until the next general election in November 1974. Funding that special election became

Figure 9.   The Recall

What it does:
- Recall is the electorate's power to remove an elected public officer from office. It can apply to any officer except a United States Representative or Senator.

How it gets on the ballot:
For statewide officers, a recall petition:
- must have voter signatures equal to 20% of the last total vote for that office.
- must have been circulated in at least 5 counties;
- for each county, signatures must be equal to at least 1% of the vote cast in that county for the office.

For state senators, assemblymen, members of the Board of Equalization, and judges of courts of appeal and trial courts, a recall petition:
- must have voter signatures equal to 20% of the last total vote for that office.

Recall supporters have 160 days to file signed petitions.

Items that appear on the recall ballot:
- "Shall _____ be recalled from the office of _____?" (Voters must answer yes or no.)
- A list of candidates is presented for the office. If the recall succeeds, the candidate with the most votes becomes the new officeholder.

How a recall passes:
- A recall election is successful when a majority of the votes cast are in its favor.

Who pays the officeholder's recall election costs:
- If a recall loses, the state treasury reimburses the officeholder under recall for his costs of the election. If the recall succeeds, the officeholder pays his own costs.

an issue; some legislative critics threatened not to appropriate the money needed to finance the election and others charged that one way the Governor could save tax dollars would be to avoid special elections.

Types of Elections

Several types of elections are conducted in California, including general, primary, and special elections. At general elections, candidates are elected to office, and voters may be asked to consider a whole series of ballot measures, such as initiative statutes and amendments and referendum measures. Primary elections are held to nominate candidates to run for office; the names of those who win nomination in the primary campaign will appear on the general election ballot. Special elections are held to take care of extraordinary needs, such as recall or special primaries.

Partisan and Nonpartisan Elections

General, primary, and special elections may be partisan or nonpartisan— that is, for some offices candidates run as the nominees of specific political parties (partisan), and for others they do not (nonpartisan). The state's partisan offices include the Governor, Lieutenant Governor, Secretary of State, Treasurer, Attorney General, Controller, State Senators, Assemblymen, and members of the Board of Equalization.

A party's candidate for a partisan office is chosen through a direct primary election in the June preceding the general election. In that same June primary, however, nonpartisan elections are also occurring. These are elections to nonpartisan offices for which parties cannot nominate candidates. When a contest for a nonpartisan office is held and one of the persons running obtains a majority of the vote cast, he is elected. But if no one gets a majority, the two individuals who received the highest number of votes face each other in a run off in the next general election. California's nonpartisan offices include the State Superintendent of Public Instruction, judges, county and city officials, and school board members. Figure 10 summarizes important points about California Elections.

Voting in California

Who can qualify as a California voter? In recent years the requirements have changed greatly because of court decisions. Much pressure has been brought to make registration to vote an easier procedure and more available to qualified citizens. The use of bilingual election officials and registrars is another much stressed reform. Figure 11 summarizes the current voting requirements.

Voters in California traditionally have faced long ballots that include candidates running for state and local offices, bond issues, initiative proposals, referendum measures, and more. The length of California ballots, and the number of candidates and ballot measures make extremely difficult the process of becoming an informed voter in the state.

Reforming the Political Process

In the early 1970s, many Californians became suspicious of the integrity of the state's electoral process. Who supported the candidates they voted

Figure 10. Elections: The Types, and When They Are Held

- *General elections:* Held during even-numbered years on the first Tuesday following the first Monday in November.
- *Primary elections:* Held during even-numbered years on the first Tuesday following the first Monday in June. Purpose is to nominate candidates to be voted for at the following general election. In a presidential election year, a presidential primary is combined with the state direct primary.
- *Special elections:* Called by the Governor for initiative and referendum proposals or for recall elections. Also called when vacancies occur in the Assembly, State Senate, or among California's representatives to the House of Representatives or the Senate of the United States. Special primaries are held for the vacant office to nominate candidates for the special election.
- *Partisan elections:* Elections to partisan offices—public offices for which political parties present their candidates.
- *Nonpartisan elections:* Elections to nonpartisan offices—public offices for which political parties cannot nominate candidates.

Figure 11. Voting Requirements

To be qualified to register to vote, one must be:
- a citizen of the United States,
- 18 years old, and
- registered for 30 days.

When one may register:
- A citizen may register to vote up to 30 days before an election.

Literacy requirements:
- English literacy is no longer required.
- The legislature *may* require literacy, but it can not discriminate against those literate in languages other than English.

for? Would a candidate, once elected, represent the public interest, or just special groups? Were political campaigns simply the product of special groups' financing and manipulation? Who was really responsible for placing measures on the ballot? Were these measures included because of public need or to meet the special needs of private groups? National and political scandals of the early 1970s surrounding the Watergate affair helped to focus attention on such questions. As a result a political reform drive emerged to ensure the integrity of the ballot, of the government process of which it was a part, and of the Constitution itself.

Reform Issues

Several specific subjects emerged for close examination and discussion. The reform of ballot pamphlet preparation discussed above was one such subject. Another was the need to limit campaign spending and to require all candidates to report more accurately and fully the names of contributors to their campaigns as well as how much each gave. It was frequently difficult to discover exactly who a given lobbyist represented, and who he was attempting to influence. Another area of concern was that of conflicts of interest—how to prevent officials from setting policy or deciding matters in which they were involved personally or financially.

Political Reform Act of 1974

As discussion of these and related issues grew, so also did pressure to clean up the entire political process. In 1973 and 1974, California's Legislature sponsored studies of political abuses. Through legislation, ballot pamphlet procedures were reformed, more informative campaign spending reports were required, and public officials had to begin filing financial disclosures or reports to avoid conflict of interest problems.

Encouraging the rush to approve such legislation was a mounting drive to place an initiative statute on the ballot to bring sweeping political reform. The Legislature and Governor—both rather reluctantly—discussed and approved legislation to bring needed reform and more importantly, to try to head off voter approval of that rather extensive initiative statute. The statute did qualify for the June 1974 primary ballot. Voters handsomely approved it. While legislative reform efforts had been remarkable, the new initiative statute, known as the Political Reform Act of 1974 or Proposition 9, was more far-reaching and thorough.[3]

Campaign Spending Report

Campaign spending was one issue covered by the reform measure. According to the Act, candidates must file financial reports before and after elections, and elected officials must file such reports during their terms of office. Such reports must list campaign contributors over $50 and how much each gave. The role of large contributors such as labor unions, corporations, citizen groups, and professional organizations in financing campaigns will now be a matter of public record. More significantly, the reports would provide a record of contributions during nonelection years.

Because the Legislature passed its own reform measure in 1973 requiring financial reports, the first reports began to be filed early in 1974. What type of information did they show, which campaign spending reformers believed to be so important? The filing of Los Angeles Mayor Thomas Bradley is a good example. In 1973, when Bradley ran for office, he relied on wealthy Democrats and liberals, and many small contributors, to finance his campaign. However, Bradley's 1974 filing revealed that during the nonelection year most of his contributions came from special interests and relatively large contributions. One labor union gave $10,000. The Los Angeles Police Protection League and United Firefighters, Los Angeles City, contributed substantial amounts. Two-thirds of the total funds collected were from contributors who gave over $500. Most of the remaining money came from contributions of over $100 each. These filings thus showed a real contrast between election year and nonelection year giving.[4]

By requiring such regular, detailed campaign fund reports, reformers hoped voters would be in a better position to judge correctly whether or not an officeholder favored those special interests who sent him campaign money, and what organizations were financing ballot measures.

Campaign Spending Limits

Another side of campaign spending considered was the rapidly increasing amounts of money being used to finance campaigns. In 1972, for example, California legislators running for office spent $8 million. The 1973 Los Angeles mayoral campaign cost the two major contestants—Bradley the winner and Yorty the loser—over $2.25 million.[5] Other candidates also ran and raised additional funds beyond this. A 1973 special spring primary and general election campaign for a vacant Senate office cost the winner about $375,000. In this campaign, special contributors put up considerable amounts: organized labor, $17,000; the California Trial Lawyers' Association, $10,000; and the California Teachers' Association, $7,500. One individual gave $5,000.

Expenses were high; postage alone cost $35,000. A major aspect of this campaign, like others, was the hiring of public relations and direct mail firms to advertise candidates. For this campaign, mailings were carefully drawn up and sent to certain community elements, including lawyers, homeowners, Jews, and real estate agents.[6]

By late 1973, major candidates for the 1974 Governor's race were

busily planning primary campaign budgets at about $1 million each—and
that was *before* active campaigning got underway for the June election.
In total, the amount of money that flowed into campaign accounts in
1973 was rather staggering. In a nonelection year, over $7 million was
collected in campaign funds. In the costly 1974 primary campaign, the
two men who won the Democratic and Republican nominations for governor spent over $2.6 million. The June primary winners of the other top
partisan offices spent nearly $2.8 million.[7]

What Good Funding Buys

The collection of large sums of money can be very important in running
a successful modern campaign. Money must be poured into television,
radio, newspaper advertising, campaign mailings, and generally into campaign accounts to finance a good public image of a candidate. In large
campaigns, a good public relations firm is needed to coordinate the
candidate's activities and the entire functioning of the campaign program.
Such firms may be a necessity for large campaigns but are very expensive.
Because all of this activity hinges on the ready availability of money,
well-financed candidates enjoy wide exposure before the public, while
financially poor campaign drives suffer from their inability to communicate
the views and images of their candidate to the public. This is true not
only for individuals' campaigns but also for ballot proposition drives.
Well-financed and well-organized proposition efforts have a much greater
chance of success in getting their positions accepted by voters than do
their underfinanced counterparts.

Spending Limits Approved

In an effort to prevent the gross expenditure of funds in campaigns, and
to avoid the extreme need of finding large contributors to fund ever-
increasing campaign budgets, the Political Reform Act placed a ceiling
on campaign spending. Specific spending limits were established for:

- all statewide offices, including Governor, Lieutenant Governor,
  Secretary of State, Treasurer, Controller, Attorney General, and
  Superintendent of Public Instruction;
- individuals seeking reelection (incumbents), to 10 percent less
  than their challengers;
- committees working to qualify ballot measures, or campaigning
  for or against propositions; and
- independent committees supporting a statewide candidate.

Public Funding of Campaigns

The Political Reform Act sought to improve the campaign funding setup
in two ways: first, to disclose the source of funding and second, to stem

the rising cost of statewide campaigns by limiting spending. The Act, though, did not touch on another solution strongly supported by some people: the proposal to have campaigns directly financed by public funds. If such a reform were adopted, no candidate would have to appeal to individuals to fund his campaign. He would avoid being indebted to any large contributor. As long as campaigns are to be privately funded, the problem of the potential influence of large contributors and their influence continues.

Historically, the most famous contributor to California electoral campaigns has been the Southern Pacific. Throughout the late nineteenth century and into the opening years of this century, the railroad was the single major source of campaign funds. Because of its tremendous financial power in campaigning, it ran state politics for many years until a political reform wave in 1910 destroyed the railroad's hold over the state. Today, no single contributor equals the power the Southern Pacific once maintained. But the example it set shows how a campaign contributor may try to take advantage and influence an officeholder.

Campaigning remains an expensive operation even with some limits. Despite the disclosure of fund sources, major contributors will still be needed. Thus, the drive for public funding of campaigns remains. The argument in favor of it is very straightforward—it would avoid financial ties creating extraordinary influences over a candidate by contributors, and would be one of the soundest investments Californians could make in improving the political process.

Conflicts of Interest Examined

In addition to problems of campaign financing, a great deal of discussion has focused on the related subject of conflicts of interest. The issue here is that an officeholder's financial and business interests and ties might be in conflict with the public interest. He might have accepted too many campaign contributions from certain lobbyists or particular special interests. Or he might be engaged in business activities with special interest elements. His real estate holdings, his business consulting activities, or his loans might bring him into a close relationship with those interests and people. Individuals who serve part-time on government boards or commissions might have to make policy or voting decisions directly affecting their full-time work. For instance, an architect or engineer serving on a zoning board or planning commission might find his clients coming to that board for decisions, and he might feel—rightly or wrongly—that his future relationship with that client could be affected by his decision.

Financial Disclosures Required

In order to uncover potential conflicts of interest, financial disclosures or reports are required of many public officers. These reports are to disclose business interests, investments, real estate holdings, and clients of public officeholders for comparison with public stands and voting records.

These financial disclosures were first required by a 1973 law, but the requirements were significantly expanded by the 1974 Political Reform Act.[8] That Act required that no public official participate in making a governmental decision in which he has a financial interest, and called upon every state and local agency to adopt its own conflict of interest code. Thus, it attacked the problem at both state and local governmental levels.

Lobbying Activity

Lobbying activities also were severely criticized and closely examined in the early 1970s. To understand why, we need to examine the purpose and role of lobbying. In the broadest sense, lobbying includes any effort to influence a public official to approve or disapprove a particular policy. Lobbyists (those who actually do the lobbying) work both on state and local government levels, attempting to persuade elected and appointed officeholders. A lobbyist may represent a single corporation, a specific industry, one special interest group, or a whole variety of interests.

The lobbyist's purpose is to represent the view of his client or employer on specific matters. To do this, he carries on a series of activities: meeting with appropriate public officials, consulting their staffs, and attending and testifying at meetings. Some lobbyists become experts in certain areas. This is especially true of those who represent a single industry, company, or special interest group. They are able to become familiar with basic issues and problems and can present strong public positions with authority. Other lobbyists prefer to avoid such public activity, and rely more on private meetings to discuss their clients' positions.

Good lobbying activity can stimulate the government process; it can provide another view of a particular issue or problem. This can have the effect of broadening the discussion, bringing more facts into consideration, and thus helping to develop sounder government policies and decisions. Good lobbying can help officials understand issues better, as well as judge more clearly the future effects of possible decisions. Lobbyist activity is found at all levels of government, but the strongest effort is directed toward state officials, especially legislators who may develop "beneficial" or "harmful" legislation that will affect the lobbyist's employer.

Criticism of Lobbying

Active lobbying means, of course, that certain special interests have their views and opinions carefully laid before the Legislature. Some critics have asserted that these interests are overrepresented in this regard. Public interest and public needs may lag behind the consideration shown towards the needs of special interest groups.

A whole series of diverse groups employ lobbyists to persuade public officials to act according to their needs. Most people think of lobbyists as individuals who represent industry or corporations; they do not always understand that many other types of groups hire representatives to promote their ideas. For example, teachers' groups employ lobbyists; so do retired people, ecologists, and animal lovers. Teachers' lobbyists are quite active in following any government decisions and legislation that affect education. Yet some teachers are highly critical of lobbying activities and of special interest groups and complain of the corruptness of such activities, perhaps not recognizing their own spokesmen as "lobbyists"—and powerful ones, at that.

Special interests are thus well represented at the doors of public officials, and legislators in particular are under a great deal of pressure to shape and approve policy or laws to meet the needs of special interests. While lobbying activity can be defended, the greater risk is that special interests may dominate the government setting. This can easily happen on particular issues because only special or minority interests may make their positions clearly known. An officeholder's problem is to determine what action is in the public interest and reconcile the special interests to that.

Lobbyist Controls Established

The Political Reform Act of 1974 sought to control lobbying activity by establishing strict guidelines for lobbyists and their work. Prior to the Act lobbyists registered with the Joint Rules Committee of the Legislature and filed reports naming the interests or persons they represented and listing expenses. Now they must register with the Secretary of State, and list those whom they represent. In addition, each lobbyist must establish a special account in which income for lobbying activity is deposited, and from which all lobbying expenses are paid. He must report the names of public officials with whom he has business dealings. He is restricted from making gifts of over $10 a month to a public official or candidate, and he is prohibited from contributing to political campaigns. The specific issues, policies, and legislation a lobbyist has sought to influence must be spelled out in reports, and the agency involved must be named. Furthermore, the lobbyist's employer must file a report indicating most expenses, gifts, and business activity involving any public officials. He, too, must indicate which issues he has sought to influence.

The requirement that such extensive records must be filed with an elected public official is an important reform. These records become public information, and they are regularly printed in legislative journals. The issues, agencies, and officials a lobbyist attempts to influence are clearly known, along with much background information on his employer.

The Fair Political Practices Commission

Ballot pamphlets, campaign spending reports, limitations on campaign expenses, lobbyists, and conflicts of interest were prime targets of the Political Reform Act of 1974. To carry out the Act's provisions and enforce its requirements, a five-member Fair Political Practices Commission was created. Two members are appointed by the Governor from different political parties. The Attorney General, Secretary of State, and Controller each appoint one member. If all three of these officials are from the same political party, the Controller has to appoint a member from a different party. No more than three members of the Commission can be from the same political party. The presence of this Commission is to ensure continually that all affected levels of government and all officials respond to this Reform Act.

The Promise of the Future

California voters in 1974 made a major step towards preserving the integrity of their Constitution. They subscribed wholeheartedly to a sweeping reform to help insure that their ballots would not contain initiative measures or candidates put there exclusively by unknown special interests. Now, through a variety of disclosure methods, those interests would be identified. California's intricate world had undergone a political housecleaning. The handling of problems and issues in the late 1970s will reveal whether the reform approved in 1974 and implemented in 1975 succeeded, whether solutions were developed in a more open manner, and were more reflective of overall public interest and public needs, rather than those of narrow special interests.

Review Questions

Why was a reform of California's constitution necessary?

How can a constitutional amendment be proposed?

What is an initiative statute, and what is an initiative constitutional amendment?

How does an initiative qualify for the ballot?

What is a referendum measure? How does it qualify for the ballot?

What is recall? How is an official recalled?

What types of elections are held in California? When are they held?

What are California voter qualifications?

What were the issues and proposals discussed about the following:
ballot pamphlet reform,
campaign spending reports,
campaign spending limits,
conflicts of interest and financial disclosures and reports, and
lobbying?

What are conflicts of interest?

What is lobbying?

List some arguments for and against lobbying.

Notes

1. Dennis Campbell, "Our Bulky Constitution—Is Pruning Season Over?" *California Journal* 4 (December, 1973): 406.

2. Campbell, "Our Bulky Constitution," pp. 404–406, 426.

3. Bruce Keppel, "Open-Government Initiative," *California Journal* 4 (November, 1973): 373–376; Louise Ma, "The New Disclosure Law," *California Journal* 5 (September, 1974): 297–300; Nancy Boyarsky, "Proposition 9: The Local-Government Loopholes," *California Journal* 5 (September, 1974): 301–303.

4. *Los Angeles Times*, March 11, 1974.

5. *Sacramento Bee*, August 20, 1973; *Los Angeles Times*, July 22, 1973.

6. *Sacramento Bee*, March 6, 1973, and April 20, 1973; *Los Angeles Times*, March 9, 1973; Nancy Boyarsky, "The Image Makers," *California Journal* 5 (May, 1974): 149–155.

7. *Sacramento Bee*, August 20, 1973; *Los Angeles Times*, July 18 and 22, 1974.

8. Bruce Keppel, "Public Disclosure and Personal Privacy—State's New Conflict-of-Interest Law," *California Journal* 5 (March, 1974): 93–94.

CHAPTER FOUR

THE EXECUTIVE

Overview

The main purpose of this chapter is to describe how the executive branch functions and what its duties are. Read carefully the charts on the Governor and the constitutional officers. From your reading you should be able to describe the main duties of each constitutional officer. As you read this chapter you should keep two major questions continually in mind:

- How much influence does the Governor have over the basic operations of the executive branch?
- In what ways can a Governor make his own philosophy felt in executive operations?

These questions are important because in forming answers to them, you will come to understand how any Governor establishes his own administration and why each has its own special character.

The task of governing the ever-changing world of California is a challenging and difficult one. To meet the challenge, a state government was created with three distinct powers or branches: legislative, executive, and judicial. Each of the three branches is theoretically to function without interfering with the powers of the other two. In practice, though, the powers of the three overlap, and at times they conflict. Even within a single branch, confusion arises occasionally. No better example exists than that of the executive branch.

The Governor and His Cabinet

Despite the fact that the California Constitution places supreme executive power in the hands of the Governor, the executive branch is in reality a diverse grouping of elected constitutional officers, appointed officials, civil service employees, and a series of independent boards and commissions. The Governor's greatest authority and power is felt in the activities and functions of the four agencies and one department (the Department of Finance) that make up what is called the administrative part of the executive branch. (See Figure 12.)

Figure 12.   The Governor

Term of office: Four years; no limit on re-election.

Qualifications: A candidate for the office of governor must be
- a voter,
- a citizen of the United States, and
- a resident of California for the five years prior to his election.

Powers and duties:
- Holds the supreme executive power in the state.
- Reports to the Legislature each year on the state's condition, and recommends changes (in the State of the State message).
- Can reorganize the executive branch, within certain limits.
- Is commander-in-chief of a state militia, which he may use to enforce the law.
- Makes appointments to boards and commissions, some of which must be confirmed by the Senate.
- Can cause the Legislature to assemble in special session.
- Can veto legislative acts.
- Can reduce or eliminate one or more items from appropriations bills, while still approving the bill in general (item veto).
- Submits to the Legislature within the first ten days of each year a budget recommending expenditures and estimating state revenues and, if necessary, suggesting new sources for additional revenues.
- Nominates and appoints judges to the Supreme Court and Courts of Appeal, subject to confirmation by the Commission on Judicial Appointments.

Vacancies in the office of Governor:
- Should the office become vacant, the order of succession is as follows: Lieutenant Governor, then President pro Tempore of the Senate, then Speaker of the Assembly, then Secretary of State, then Attorney General, then Treasurer, then Controller. If none of these can serve, the Legislature designates by law a person to serve.
- Whenever the Governor leaves the state temporarily, the above-named officers serve as Acting Governor, in the order stated.

- The question of the existence of a vacancy or the Governor's temporary disability may be raised by a Commission composed of the President pro Tempore of the Senate, the Speaker of the Assembly, President of the University of California, Chancellor of the State Colleges, and the Director of Finance. The California Supreme Court has exclusive jurisdiction over the final decision as to whether a vacancy or disability exists in fact.

Impeachment:
- The Governor may be impeached by the Assembly and tried by the Senate.
- A two-thirds vote of the Senate membership is required for conviction.

Agency Secretaries

Each of the four agencies is headed by a Secretary who oversees the functioning of the various departments within his agency. His job is to keep communications open among those departments, between himself and the department heads, and between them and the Governor. This open flow of communication is important so that policy may be carried out or changed if necessary, and so that coordinated activity will result from the work of the individual departments. Thus, the director of a department actually supervises the work of that department, and the Secretary attempts to guarantee the smooth operation of *all* the departments in the agency.

Each Secretary is responsible to the Governor and has the following duties:

- reports to him on the activities of the departments in his agency,
- recommends policy for the agency or a specific department,
- recommends legislation to aid the development of programs in the agency, and
- accounts for the budgetary matters of his agency.

Basically, agency Secretaries provide the Governor with essential information on the workings of state government (including its successes and problems) and identify subjects and areas needing development.

The concept of agency Secretaries developed under former Governor Edmund G. (Pat) Brown, Sr. Because there were so many departments it was impossible to lead them all and achieve active unity among them. During Brown's term, departments were grouped under eight agencies to improve efficiency, give direction to the executive setting, better coordinate policy, and improve decision making.

When Ronald Reagan entered office, his keynote was streamlining and combining. The Reagan administration worked to merge departments and to consolidate efforts. This practice continued to the end of his administration. One of the early changes Reagan made was to reduce the agencies from eight to four.

Cabinet Personnel

The Director of Finance and the four agency Secretaries—the Secretary of Agriculture and Services, the Secretary of Business and Transportation, the Secretary of Resources, the Secretary of Health and Welfare—sit as the members of the Governor's cabinet along with the Governor's chief aide, his Executive Assistant. In addition to these individuals, elected constitutional officers such as the Lieutenant Governor may be included in cabinet discussions, as well as key members of the Governor's immediate staff.

The cabinet idea actually emerged during the administration of Governor Edmund (Pat) Brown. Because Brown found a council made up of department heads too cumbersome an operation for deliberation, he selected a small group of his top administrators for such meetings. When Governor Reagan followed Brown into office, he formalized the cabinet idea.

The Cabinet's Importance

The cabinet, then, is a basic element within the executive branch that directly aids the Governor in guiding state operations. As an advisory and a policy-making body, it coordinates the thinking and the approach of the Governor and the executive departments on state operations. It aims to provide effective management controls and careful administration through the formulation of thoughtfully developed policy. In cabinet meetings, advice on the budget is sought, the direction and tone of state programs are reviewed in the light of the Governor's thinking and philosophy, the policies, planning, and operation of the four agencies are coordinated, and current legislation is considered so that the basis for a decision to approve or veto may be established. The cabinet emphasizes a team approach to administration and provides the communication link among the departments, agencies, and the Governor.

While the cabinet has a vital role in establishing a direction and tone to any administration, one must not overlook the importance of the Governor's own personal staff, which conducts studies, outlines potential policy positions, and does much basic preparatory work for the Governor.

Figure 13. The Governor and His Cabinet Officers

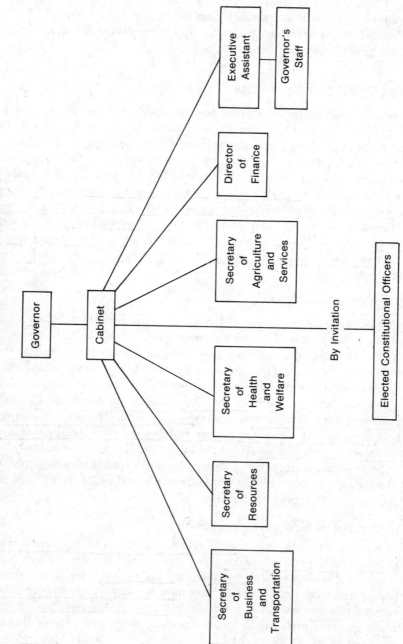

In a sense, the staff may be of equal if not greater importance than the cabinet in helping to establish and determine policy outlines for the Governor. For most issues, it is probably the personal staff that determines basic policy positions.[1]

The Department of Finance

The four Secretaries head agencies composed of departments that are actually administered and run by their particular department heads. The Director of Finance has a somewhat different position; he is in charge of a single department—the Department of Finance—and he is the Governor's chief advisor on financial matters. The Department of Finance is the body that continually surveys state financial activity and economic development and supervises the implementation of the Governor's fiscal (financial) policy. The Department's major responsibility is to keep the Governor aware of the state of California's economic well-being, and of the condition of the state's finances. It also analyzes the financial impact of pending legislation.

Budget Planning

One of the most important duties of the Department of Finance is to produce the budget that the Governor presents to the Legislature. To do this, the Department brings together budgetary requests from various state departments, and puts together a budget in accord with the policies determined by the cabinet and Governor, and within the limits of anticipated state income. Perhaps the Department's most difficult task is to estimate future state income, and then once the state budget is adopted, to make sure that the actual income matches the estimated income upon which the budget was based. At the same time this Department regularly inspects different agencies' and departments' expenditures to determine that they are in line with the administration's established spending policy, and agree with legal requirements.

Restrictions on Revenues and Spending

A major problem is that much budget planning and state spending is required and restricted by law, and thus is actually determined *before* the budget is written. For instance, gas tax revenues constitute a huge part of the state's income, but they must be spent according to constitutional requirements. As a result, little true flexibility remains in budget planning. This problem becomes especially significant during times of economic crises. In late 1970 and early 1971, for example, state revenues were running behind previous estimates, and the Governor had to make a series of cutbacks in state spending to match the declining revenues. At that time, out of a $6.5 billion budget, all but about $1.8 billion was legally restricted. Yet a savings of $250 million was needed to balance decreased revenues. All the cuts, therefore, had to come from this relatively small part (roughly one-third) of the total budget.

Because little flexibility exists within the budget, any Governor rapidly discovers that it is difficult to alter many of California's programs and accomplish major changes. Thus, because a 1933 constitutional amendment guaranteed gas tax revenues and restricted their use until 1974, rapid transit and other alternative transportation methods had to be financed out of other revenue sources, while at the same time highway construction had to continue. When voters in 1974 approved a change in the use of gas tax monies for purposes other than highway construction, part of the income could go to the development of mass transit, but even so, these tax revenues are severely restricted and the Governor still has little say in their expenditure.

Analyst's Challenges

The budget planning work of the Department of Finance reflects the interests and goals of the Governor and his staff. Both in constructing the budget and in estimating state income, the Department's work conforms to the current Governor's view.[2] The Department's activities thus can be very partisan at times—that is, they may reflect the Governor's political views and those of his party, and as a result the Department's findings and activities may conflict with that of another source—the Legislative Analyst. The Analyst's work will be discussed in Chapter Five, but it is important to note here that that office carries on many of the same tasks as the Department of Finance. However, the Analyst is hired by the Legislature, not the Governor. His office tends to examine the budget and the Department's reports from a different point of view, one that is often critical of the Department's work, and thus of the Governor's policies. Such conflict has led some Governors to challenge the impartiality of the Analyst's reports, and to charge that office with engaging in partisan criticism—especially when the Legislature's majority and the Governor are from different parties.

State Agencies and Departments

Each of the four agency Secretaries supervises the activity of many departments. For instance, the authority of the Secretary in charge of the Resources Agency extends over the previously discussed Department of Water Resources, the Air Resources Board, the State Water Resources Control

Figure 14. The Executive Branch—California State Government

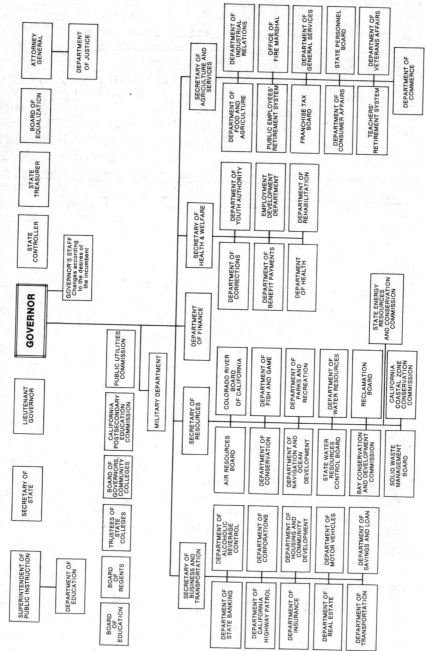

Board, the Bay Area Conservation and Development Commission, and the State Energy Resources and Conservation Commission, as well as several other boards and departments. These departments and boards carry on a wide range of activities. Some of them will be discussed to illustrate the general functioning of the agencies and their various departments.

Department of Water Resources

The Department of Water Resources coordinates the use of the state's water. As described earlier, its work includes the conservation of water, the investigation of new sources, the distribution of water, flood control, the use of waste water, desalinization planning (removal of salt from water), use of geothermal water (hot water and steam from inside the earth), and the protection of ground water. An important aspect of this Department's work was the development and publication of the California Water Plan in 1957, establishing a framework for long-range planning to meet California water needs. The Department's implementation of the plan has involved not only actual construction but also a series of ongoing studies judging the Project's impact, determining how best to continue it, adjusting facilities to California's changing needs. For instance, a 1970 study revealed that California's population growth rate was decreasing, and that therefore, the state's water needs would increase at a far slower rate than previously thought. Thus, construction could be slowed, and the overall plan for the Project reassessed. The Project simply redistributes water from the north to the south, rather than creating any new supplies. Perhaps, because the growth rate is slowing, there is now less need for additional construction work on northern California rivers. That is welcome news to those who have supported "wild rivers" legislation to protect north coastal rivers from being used by the Project, and to others who have opposed the construction of a peripheral canal in the delta.

State Water Resources Control Board

The Department of Water Resources concentrates on the *use* of water; the State Water Resources Control Board (SWRCB), as noted earlier, focuses on water *quality* under the provision of the Porter–Cologne Water Quality Control Act. The SWRCB and nine California Regional Water Quality Control Boards work to reduce water pollution through the use of water quality control plans. Thus, within the Resources Agency, the Department of Water Resources and the SWRCB complement each other to help assure Californians of an adequate and relatively pure water supply.

Air Resources Board: The Impact of the Energy Crisis

Also within the Resources Agency is the very important Air Resources Board (ARB), which coordinates all air pollution control activities in

Figure 15.   The Resources Agency

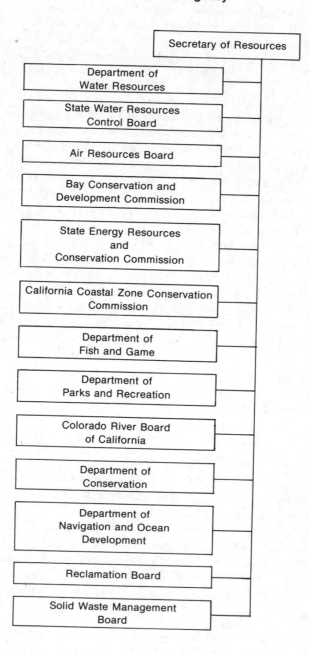

California. The ARB provides assistance to local air pollution control districts and acts directly, when necessary, to enforce pollution regulations.

The drive to clean up California's air suffered a sharp setback in late 1973, when the energy crisis took hold and gasoline supplies dwindled. The ARB came under intense pressure to repeal a previous requirement that all 1966–70 model cars be equipped with antismog devices. The installation schedule was to go into effect on January 1, 1974, but when the energy crisis hit, then-Governor Ronald Reagan felt that these devices would increase gasoline consumption, and he asked the ARB to suspend or delay its schedule.

When it appeared that the ARB might not go along with this suggestion, Reagan took action. One position on the ARB was vacant, and another member was retiring; another unexpectedly (and apparently from pressure) resigned, and a fourth member (the only woman) was fired. She had steadfastly opposed any changes in the ARB's position on requirements. The Governor quickly filled the four positions, and in December 1973, the new Board voted to suspend the controversial requirement. Environmentalists cried foul and brought suit to reverse the action. The California Supreme Court ruled in June 1974 that the ARB had exceeded its authority, and thus had to revoke its suspension.

The Legislature then moved to change the antismog device requirement. In late summer 1974, it passed legislation that removed the provision requiring installation of these devices on 1966–70 cars throughout California, except for six counties in southern California where air pollution was so serious. In the rest of California the antismog devices will be required only upon transfer of ownership or new registration. Despite the fact this new law did not take effect until January 1, 1975, the ARB quickly modified its requirement so that the legislative modification became effective at once.

The Governor's obvious manipulation of the ARB generated great criticism of the Board. With an ARB so easily open to pressure, how was clean air ever going to appear over the state? Several suggestions were made to strengthen the Board, to make it more independent, and to remove it from the Governor's direct control.

Thus, three divisions of the Resources Agency became quite controversial in the early 1970s. Environmentalists were highly critical of the ARB's general lack of effectiveness; they wondered if the SWRCB was firmly requiring quality water; and they criticized the Water Resources Department's plans for increased construction.

Coordination of Departments

Even though departments within each agency act independently of one another in carrying out their duties, a great deal of coordination does exist. Several departments may be involved in supporting the same project. For example, both the Department of Fish and Game and the Department of Parks and Recreation played a significant part in the California Water Project. As construction of Project dams drew to a close and lakes began to fill, the Department of Fish and Game began the work of expanding and developing fish hatcheries in order to keep the lakes stocked with fish. At the same time the Department of Parks and Recreation undertook the planning of a $54 million recreation development program at Project sites.

New Departments Created

Department of Transportation

Two new departments emerged within two other agencies in 1973. The Department of Transportation appeared within the Business and Transportation Agency. The purpose of this new Department, as noted in Chapter Two, was to improve the quality of transportation, explore a variety of solutions to transportation problems, and select for development the modes or types of transportation best suited to meet each one. The idea for the creation of the new Department came from the studies and proposals made in 1968 by a special committee formed by the Governor and called the Governor's Task Force on Transportation, although the legislation that created the Department was not signed by the Governor until December 1972. The Transportation Department is to provide coordination and cooperation between governments, and to encourage and support regional transportation agencies and systems. The Department is to emphasize a multimodal approach; mass transit systems, air transportation systems, and highway development are to be equally evaluated and encouraged. While the concern of the Department of Transportation is moving people, it must consider a number of aspects in its planning. The social impact of a transportation system must be weighed equally with its economic and environmental effects.

Department of Health

Just as important as the appearance of the Department of Transportation as a reflection of the trends and tone of the 1970s was a newly created department within the Health and Welfare Agency. In 1973, this agency was pushing towards general reform. The first significant change was the establishment of a new Department of Health, created by combining three other departments, in a major effort to provide better coordination of health programs, less duplication of services, and higher quality health

Figure 16.   The Business and Transportation Agency

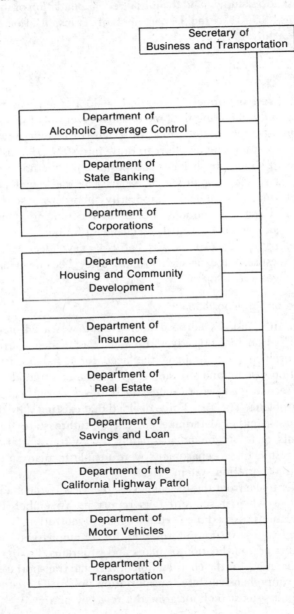

services. This new Department was the result of much work, many hearings, several task force studies, and the initial recommendation of the Legislative Analyst in 1967. Like the Department of Transportation, it appeared officially on July 1, 1973.[3]

Task Forces

A major interest of former Governor Ronald Reagan was reorganizing, stimulating and redirecting the tone of state government. From the outset of his administration in 1967, Reagan sought to involve new individuals in government studies, in an effort to draw into state administration what he considered absent—fresh ideas and businesslike methods. He used the task force (a special committee of experts) as the vehicle for bringing new people into government temporarily in order to study particular problems and suggest solutions. Based on recommendations from task forces, new policies were outlined and changes proposed. The use of special committees of outside experts was hardly a new idea. What was new was the widespread use of such groups. They became a characteristic of Reagan's years as Governor.[4]

Task Force on Transportation

The Governor's Task Force on Transportation was a 24-member group assigned two principal objectives. First, it was to define existing transportation problems, emphasizing the need for a balanced, multimodal transportation system, and stressing the importance of good overall planning. The second goal was to suggest a state organizational structure to solve the problems. The Task Force decided that existing state departments were unable to either determine current or future state transportation requirements, or to obtain and adequately review transportation information. As a result, these departments were unable to plan an all-inclusive statewide transportation system.

In order to confront these weaknesses, the Task Force made a number of suggestions when it submitted its report in November 1968. Those recommendations stressed the need for better organization, for the regular collection of transportation information, for an emphasis on better planning, for greater coordination of plans and programs, for regional transportation planning, for the coordination of regional transportation districts, and for a comprehensive state transportation policy. The committee felt that state policy must be built around a few key aims:

- to develop *all* modes of transportation to serve a variety of needs,

- to encourage transportation research and
- to reevaluate present transportation regulations in order to end unnecessary restrictions and encourage greater transportation development.

In the years following 1968 when the study was made, transportation became an increasingly important problem. To handle this growing crisis, the executive administration was reorganized. Much of that reorganization was based on the ideas presented in the Task Force report. The Department of Transportation was an outgrowth of this effort to solve transportation problems, based on ideas presented by the Task Force.

The Department of Transportation, therefore, is a useful example of several aspects of California government. Its origins may be traced to a task force, which is significant in light of the Reagan interest in these groups. Also, the Department brings together a new effort to develop a multimodal approach to transportation. Its approach is based not only on mobility goals, but also on social, economic, and environmental considerations. This approach took on special significance in 1973 as the Department began functioning. At that time the federal Environmental Protection Agency was discussing gas rationing, raising the gas tax to cut down on consumption, limiting car use, and closing areas to motor vehicles in an effort to control smog.

Task Force on Law Enforcement

Another task force suggested the establishment of a new cabinet-level body to be called the Public Safety Agency. This recommendation came from the Governor's Task Force on Law Enforcement Problems, which began its work in the fall of 1972 and issued its report early in 1973. Concentrating on crime control measures and including in its study law enforcement as well as court problems, the Task Force suggested that California needed a better system of management in the area of public safety. This objective was to be accomplished by regrouping several existing departments and offices under a new agency. By having the agency Secretary in the cabinet, the task force felt the issue of public safety would be given more attention.[5]

Task Force on Tax Reduction

In addition, former Governor Reagan was much concerned with tax revenues—specifically, with the ever-increasing taxes burdening Californians. In 1972, a Task Force on Tax Reduction began its work, focusing primarily on how to control government spending, in order to limit the amount of an individual's income that the state taxed and control constantly increasing taxes. The group's startling recommendation, which Reagan approved and announced in February 1973 was a tax ceiling to be written into the Constitution, effectively forcing a cut in government spending, and protecting the overburdened taxpayer. The Legislature proved hostile to the whole idea, and did not recommend it as a constitutional amendment to the voters for their approval.

Reagan then pushed to get his proposal on the ballot through the initiative process. Intense criticism mounted against the idea of a tax ceiling. To meet that criticism and attract enough attention to obtain the necessary signatures to qualify the measure as an initiative amendment for the ballot, Reagan began a personal campaign. In radio commercials and in speeches, he said the initiative expressed his conservative philosophy toward government, and hailed it as a marvelously simple yet effective way of halting both the growth of government and the decline of individual freedom.

This initiative illustrates several aspects of how a Governor uses his executive position. First, a task force proposed the plan, a fine example of Reagan's use of such bodies to advise on executive matters. Second, this task force was composed of individuals who were basically in agreement with the Governor's conservative view of the tax matters. Thus, the Task Force on Tax Reduction produced suggestions the Governor approved and urged. Third, when the Legislature did not immediately support the tax reduction idea, the Governor put himself and his office into the campaign to qualify the measure for the ballot. The Task Force, its recommendations, the use of the initiative process, and the direct involvement of the Governor's office all interacted to support a proposal basic to the Governor's philosophy of government.

Executive Influence and Centralization

Not only can a Governor put the power and prestige of his office directly behind a proposal and campaign for it, but the entire administrative machinery under the Governor's direction can also work as a powerful lobby for specific proposals. Reagan's lobbying effort for the tax reduction initiative is a good example of how the executive branch can mobilize itself to action. While this instance specifically involves the Governor's office and the use of his authority to form a task force group, pay it, and then pressure for approval of its proposals, a much broader executive lobbying effort is continually underway in work with the Legislature.

Unification of State Agencies

Executive agency and department lobbying was an activity refined by the Reagan administration but begun during the term of Governor Edmund

G. (Pat) Brown, Sr. What Brown painfully and disastrously discovered was that various executive departments tended to press separately for legislation, sometimes conflicting with one another over the need and desirability of specific proposals and legislative bills. The Brown administration found it difficult if not impossible to present a unified view and a single voice to the Legislature when state departments publicly argued among themselves. The result was the executive's inability to obtain legislative goals. Brown clearly saw the need for centralization and coordination of departmental action and began a reform effort to tighten up executive action. That effort was continued and formalized under Reagan. Today, the legislative needs of agencies and departments are directed through the Governor's office for review and coordination, so that any conflicts and problems may be corrected there *before* proposals are presented to the Legislature.

Furthermore, other legislation that is introduced is reviewed systematically by the Governor's office, and the opinions of selected departments and agencies are gathered so that the administration already has the necessary background and can take a position if it is enacted and sent to the Governor for his signature.

The Governor: California's Biggest Lobbyist

The actual lobbying effort starts once legislation is reviewed and a position decided. Specified individuals or legislative coordinators within the Governor's office and within appropriate departments proceed to push for or against legislation. A Governor, in this role, becomes California's most powerful individual lobbyist, and these various coordinators are his agents. On occasion, the Governor himself may speak out to mobilize public support, personally discuss the merits of his position with key legislators and, if necessary, threaten to veto unacceptable bills. This action, combined with executive departments speaking as one voice, enables the executive branch to present and support its position forcefully and effectively.

An additional factor aids these executive efforts. Not only do department representatives speak with unity but they also speak as experts on their particular subjects. That is very important in arguing and defending legislation before a legislative committee. Few opponents can bring together the resources of a state department in providing the research studies and information so important to a careful, thoughtful presentation.[6]

Publicity on Executive Departments

Other techniques are used to present the Governor's position and that of executive agencies and departments. Information officers within each of the cabinet-level agencies and within each department act to publicize the work and policy of the agency or department. Much of this activity is centrally directed by a member of the Governor's staff. The effect of such action is to insure that the position of the executive branch on certain matters and its accomplishments are adequately displayed and presented to the news media. During Reagan's administration, tapes for radio broadcast were carefully prepared, and any radio station in the state could call for free news releases of happenings within the executive branch. Those free tapes could then be broadcast directly to listeners.

The significance of this service and these information officers is that they present packaged and easily broadcast views of subjects the executive branch believes need communicating to the public, either to achieve support for some proposal or to call attention to success in a particular area. The more effective such an operation is, the greater the influence of the executive agencies and departments.

The Governor's position also can be communicated through the skillful use of the State of the State message, which he makes at the beginning of each legislative session or in special messages sent to the Legislature. Sometimes those speeches may merely note accomplishments. They can, however, be used to call attention to particular problems, and may detail specific suggested legislative action. These messages and the publicity they receive enable a Governor to draw attention to his views, his philosophy, and his approach to solving problems facing the state.

Centralization in the Governor's Office

During the Reagan administration, a significant shift took place in the Governor's personal influence and mode of leadership. Under Governor Pat Brown a centralization trend had emerged. Brown organized departments under agency heads and originated the cabinet idea, but he did not formalize this setup, so it remained quite flexible. That meant Brown remained readily available to meet with department directors, agency heads, and legislators to discuss problems, issues, and legislation. Legislators—both Republican and Democrat—found him willing to sit down and review problems and bargain and compromise if necessary. Furthermore, his cabinet and staff never became such a small, tightly knit group that he was isolated from other state officials. He worked with his staff, cabinet, and a council with a larger representation of important executive officials.

In marked contrast, Ronald Reagan's administration was much more ideologically oriented. Reagan's adherence to his own political philosophy made it more difficult for outsiders to deal with him, and made negotiations almost impossible. He and his staff insisted that issues, problems, and legislation be considered along rather rigid philosophical lines. In addition, his executive organization was streamlined and consolidated, leaving only a small inner group of immediate staff and cabinet. This advisory group

tended to shield and isolate Reagan from other people. Department directors found it difficult to schedule meetings with the Governor, and in
general to know what was going on. Legislators too were isolated. Brown
had enjoyed good relations with Republican and Democratic legislators;
Reagan had poor relations with both. Neither Democrats nor Republicans
had free access to the Governor to review issues and iron out legislation
problems. When discussions did take place, many felt that the Governor's
ideological or philosophical views inhibited the openness needed to resolve
problems. Bargaining was difficult because the Governor wanted conces-
sions, not negotiation, and threatened to veto the legislation if the conces-
sions were not forthcoming.

During Reagan's term, much legislation was written in the Governor's
office. In meetings for that purpose, 12 to 15 people including the Governor, his staff, representatives of the Senate and Assembly, and both Republicans and Democrats, met behind closed doors to work out the details
of particular legislation. Later, when public hearings were held in the
Legislature on these measures, they were meaningless because the Governor
and his staff refused to accept changes. Medi-Cal amendments in 1971,
welfare reform in 1971, tax relief and school financing in 1972, and welfare
support changes at the 1973 special legislative session were all decided
during such private, secret meetings.

Thus, under Governor Reagan, centralization in the executive branch
was carried to its logical conclusion. The purpose of this concentration
of power was to speed up things and make operations more efficient.
But in the process both legislative and public involvement were severely
weakened.[7]

Elected Constitutional Officers

Division of Authority

A major problem facing any Governor is that much of his power has
been separated from his office and divided among a series of elected
officers—the Lieutenant Governor, Attorney General, Treasurer, Controller, Secretary of State, and Superintendent of Public Instruction. Two
of those officers are of special significance. The Attorney General and
the Superintendent of Public Instruction both directly supervise the activities of major influential departments that are not under direct gubernatorial
supervision: the Departments of Justice and of Education.

The power of these elected officials presents a problem for the Governor because they are independent of his authority. They may reject his
opinions and policies and establish and pursue their own goals. Further-

more, their independence is enlarged because they have direct access to the Legislature in requesting funds and in suggesting their own programs. Therefore, to produce some coordination, good communication between these officers and the Governor is vitally needed. A major responsibility of the Governor's staff is to achieve and maintain such communication. The most important communication links are those with the Attorney General and Superintendent of Public Instruction, because they control independent departments that are not directly represented in the Governor's cabinet. The Governor's staff, therefore, includes an Education Advisor and a Legal Affairs Secretary, who provide the necessary coordination between these departments and the Governor, though a close relationship may still not exist between them.

Another difficulty in the relationship between the Governor and these officers is that each campaigns separately for office. In an election the voters may select persons from different political parties to serve in these offices. Even the Lieutenant Governor, who is the second highest state officer, may be from a different party. Occasionally, even when they are from the same party, the Governor and Lieutenant Governor do not share the same ideas about governing the state. During his second term, Reagan was faced with a Secretary of State [Edmund G. (Jerry) Brown, Jr.] who was not only a Democrat, but was also the son of a former Democratic Governor and hoped to become Governor himself.

The ambitions of elected officials further complicate the division of authority in the executive branch. In the 1974 gubernatorial primary race, for example, three of the constitutional officers became rivals for the nomination. The Secretary of State, Lieutenant Governor, and Controller all began charting the opening efforts of their gubernatorial primary campaigns in 1973, so they were not really a part of the Governor's team. They were not prepared to bow to his ideas and follow his particular policies, because they were going to have to campaign on their own records and achievements, not the Governor's.[8]

Some critics believe that the problem with California's executive branch is that it is too divided and needs to be more unified. Several suggestions have been made as to how such unification could be accomplished. One recommendation is that Governor and Lieutenant Governor be elected as a team, rather than separately, in order to provide more effective leadership in state government. Another is that many officers that are now elected instead be appointed by the Governor. This would bring all the major functions of the executive branch under the direction of the Governor. Supporters of the present system, however, defend it by arguing that the independence of these officers assures less graft and corruption, and provides an effective check on the Governor's power.

**Figure 17.   The Other Constitutional Officers and
Board of Equalization Members**

Lieutenant Governor
Secretary of State
Superintendent of Public
  Instruction
Controller

Attorney General
Treasurer
Board of Equalization
  (4 members)

Term of Office:
- Same as Governor: 4 years with no limit to re-election.
- Term begins on the Monday after the January 1 following
  election.

Qualifications:
Same as Governor:
- A voter,
- A citizen of the United States,
- A resident of California for the five years before election.

When elected:
- At the same time as the Governor: at general elections every
  four years.

Recall:
- All are subject to the recall process.

Impeachment:
- All are subject to impeachment by the Assembly to be tried by
  the Senate.

Lieutenant Governor

If a Governor dies, is disabled, or is absent from the state, the Lieutenant Governor is the officer who succeeds him. Other than that, his duties as described by the Constitution are very brief. In fact, his only other stated responsibility is to serve as President of the Senate, where he casts the deciding vote in the event of a tie. He does serve on various boards, such as the Regents of the University of California, the State Lands Commission, and the Trustees of the California State Universities and Colleges.

Because a Lieutenant Governor has few formal responsibilities, his relationship with the Governor is highly important. The Governor can assign him additional duties. For example, Reagan's second Lieutenant Governor, Ed Reinecke, enjoyed friendly relations with the Governor, and Reagan transferred more responsibility to the office. Reinecke thus assumed a more active role in state affairs, enabling him to become more widely known than most Lieutenant Governors. For example, he became involved in task force work and directed a 1973 Task Force on Local Government Reform.[9]

The assignment of extra responsibilities to the office of Lieutenant Governor is important if he is truly to become involved in the executive process. Thus, the personality and energy of the officeholder determine the range of influence he will have. This is also true of the other elected executive officers, particularly the Secretary of State, who also has few constitutionally assigned major duties.

Secretary of State

The Secretary of State is charged with record keeping functions. One basic duty is to maintain a log of all official acts of both the Governor and Legislature. He also keeps a record of the articles of incorporation of all California corporations, is in charge of the state archives, and receives for filing financing statements for credit information.

The Secretary of State is also California's chief election officer. His office enforces election laws and their requirements, and arranges for the printing of state ballot pamphlets. It is to the office of the Secretary of State that petitions for initiative, referendum, and recall action are submitted for certification that they contain the proper number of signatures to qualify for the ballot. The Secretary then submits qualified items to the voters, and afterwards certifies the results of the elections. He also issues certificates of election to officeholders and prepares the official statement of voting results on state elections.

For nearly 60 years the office of Secretary of State was held by two members of the Jordan family—first the father for 29 years, and then the son for 28 years. Their work attracted little attention, and most Californians believed the position to be a quiet, uninteresting one. With the election of Edmund G. (Jerry) Brown, Jr., to the office in 1970, that view changed. Brown quickly demonstrated that he intended to be an outspoken, vigorous officeholder. He began his term by launching an investigation into anonymous contributions to finance a campaign against a statewide ballot measure that would have permitted gas tax revenues to be used to provide smog control and mass transit systems. Following the investigation, a lawsuit was filed, and the anonymous contributors emerged to reveal their support. Brown thus showed that the Secretary of State could have a greater role in state affairs. In 1973, one person admitted that he was running for the office of Secretary of State because Brown had demonstrated that a person filling the position could be an effective and visible member of the executive branch.

Much of Brown's interest focused on election laws and their enforcement. He was interested in revising the format of the ballot pamphlet and upgrading the quality of the material included in it, primarily with the idea of making the content more understandable to the average voter. Brown also was concerned with improving the procedure for filing campaign contribution reports, and he proposed much stricter reporting methods. Furthermore, he objected strongly to the practice of paying people to circulate initiative petitions, feeling that this only helped place many unwanted measures on the ballot. For all these reasons, he supported the Political Reform Act of 1974. Brown was also interested in using new methods to expand voter registration.

In general, the most important point to note about this office is that during the early 1970s, the Secretary of State as an official became more widely known. Brown's actions, more than any other single factor, made the office more visible and newsworthy.[10]

Controller

Another constitutional position not always well known is that of the Controller, the state's chief fiscal officer. He has several important responsibilities, including the accounting and paying out of money. The control of all state accounts, the examining of claims against the state, the issuing of warrants to pay the state's obligations from the treasury, and the preparation of the state's payroll are some of the major activities of this office. The controller also reports on state and local finances, and advises local governments on budgetary matters and the collection of taxes. The fact that he is elected rather than appointed provides an independence from the Governor that increases the believability of his advising, reporting, and examining procedures.

The functions of the Office of Controller are different from those of the Department of Finance, and they serve to provide a check on the reporting of that Department. The Controller's office also collects some taxes, such as inheritance taxes. In addition to these responsibilities, the Controller is a member of a series of boards and commissions dealing with financial matters. He serves, for instance, as chairman of the Franchise Tax Board, which collects income taxes and corporation franchise taxes. He is also a member of the very important Board of Equalization, which collects several taxes, including the gas tax and sales tax, and attempts to equalize local property taxes on a statewide basis.

The Controller serves as well as chairman of the State Lands Commission. This important but little known body controls the state's public lands, the most significant of which are the coastal tidelands. These tidelands are leased by the Commission to oil and utility companies for oil and gas production. It was the State Lands Commission that closed the Santa Barbara Channel to new drilling following a 1969 oil spill on federal land. In late 1973, after a five-year closure to new development, the Commission approved reopening the Santa Barbara Channel and other southern California areas to new drilling. Drilling applications would have to be approved by both this Commission and the regional coastline conservation commissions before actual drilling could begin.

Controller's Importance.   The individual serving as Controller has a vital function in accounting, examining, and paying out state funds. As a member of boards that administer state revenues, he also has important revenue collection responsibilities beyond the duties specifically assigned to him. The significant fact that the office is elective enables the holder to function independently of department groups under the Governor's authority.[11]

In 1973, for example, when a dispute arose over the funding of former Governor Reagan's Task Force on Tax Reduction, the Controller withheld payment until the matter could be resolved. The charge against Governor Reagan's office was the improper use and transfer of funds. The money being used to pay the Task Force had been appropriated for use by the Department of Human Resources and the Department of Social Welfare. One Task Force member's salary was paid with money from the unemployment compensation disability fund—which is supposed to be used to pay disabled individuals. The Governor's office insisted that no appropriated funds had been misused, but the Controller—perhaps in part because he was an elected and not an appointed officer of the Governor—refused to issue further warrants for payment. The Controller's office waited for the Attorney General's office to study the situation and issue an opinion on the legality of payment. The Attorney General's office decided that payment could be made, but the Governor's office would first have to show that the expenditures were proper ones for the accounts from which they were to be taken. The Governor's office first withdrew its request for payment, and then indicated it would repay some of the earlier funds spent. Three constitutional officers became involved, and the value of having an elected official who is independent of gubernatorial authority was evident.[12]

Treasurer

When the Controller's office issues warrants against the treasury, it is authorizing payment from the funds held by the state Treasurer. The

Treasurer acts as banker for the state, and maintains the accounts in which state funds are deposited. In addition, he invests certain state monies. He chairs the Pooled Money Investment Board, which also includes the Controller and Director of Finance. The Board determines the amount of money available for investment, and the Treasurer then makes the actual investment. These investment activities earn millions of dollars for the state.

Besides paying current state bills and investing funds, the Treasurer also sells bonds. After voters approve state bond issues, the Treasurer's office attempts to sell those bond issues under the best available financial conditions. In short, the California Treasurer is primarily a banker, and the Treasurer's office performs banking activities for the state.[13]

In contrast to the somewhat narrow duties and responsibilities and small staffs of the Lieutenant Governor, Secretary of State, Controller, and Treasurer, stand the positions of the Attorney General and the Superintendent of Public Instruction. These two officers not only have more extensive responsibilities but also direct their own departments.

Attorney General

As California's chief law officer, the Attorney General is responsible for seeing that the laws of the state are strictly enforced in the same manner throughout the state. He has direct supervision over California law enforcement officers and agencies, including the work of district attorneys, sheriffs, and police chiefs. In order to fulfill his duties, the Attorney General may require that these officials report on the investigation, detection, prosecution, and punishment of crime within their particular areas. If he believes a state law is not being adequately enforced in any county, he has the responsibility to intervene and prosecute the violations. Furthermore, he assists district attorneys in carrying out the duties of their office.

The Attorney General also heads the Department of Justice, which is in charge of all the state's legal business. The Department represents all state officers, agencies, departments, and boards who do not have their own legal advisors, and assists these groups in legally fulfilling their duties. One important function of the Department of Justice is to issue legal opinions when requested, on questions of law that affect the work of state officers, agencies, and boards. For example, in the dispute described above over the use of funds to pay the Tax Reduction Task Force, the Controller's office had asked the Department of Justice for an opinion. Such opinions are binding and have the force of law until the courts review the matter.

The Department of Justice

To coordinate the Attorney General's activities and duties and that of the Department of Justice, the Department is split into a series of divisions.

These divisions focus on civil law, criminal law, consumer interests, environmental problems, the collection of information (such as fingerprints) to aid in criminal investigation and identification, organized crime activities, and narcotics control. In general, the work of the Department directly aids law enforcement by assisting state and local law enforcement officers in their tasks, and provides advice, investigation, and identification services. When necessary, of course, it also handles lawsuits for the state.

The Department also undertakes to study necessary changes in California law and promote legislation to accomplish that change. It actively carries on independent studies and lobbying activities to bring needed improvements through new legislation.

Because the work of this office includes so many state officials, agencies, departments, and local officials, its activities are broader and its work has a greater and more immediate effect than that of other constitutional officers. This same point holds true for the work of the Superintendent of Public Instruction.[14]

Superintendent of Public Instruction

The Superintendent of Public Instruction is the only nonpartisan position among the state constitutional offices. The Superintendent directs the activities of the Department of Education and implements the policies and regulations established by the State Board of Education, the governing and policy-making body for the Department. The Superintendent serves as the Board's secretary and is its executive officer in carrying out decisions.

The work of the Superintendent and the Department of Education is highly important; together they have charge of the California public school system, including its elementary and secondary schools. Over 1,000 school districts fall under the Department's supervision. Even though each school district is independent and provides its own leadership, it is part of the public school system and must respond to the leadership of the state Department. The Department provides professional guidance, assistance, and coordination in the education of 4.6 million children, a task toward which the state contributes over $2 billion worth of aid.

Changing Trends in California Education. The trend and problem in California education following World War II was fantastic growth. Children flooded California classrooms. Enrollment tripled between 1945 and 1970, but now the school population is leveling off. The major challenge is no longer the increasing numbers of children. Now the emphasis is on improving the quality of educational programs and modernizing curriculum. Because educational costs have risen so rapidly, the strongest and most productive programs must be supported and weaker ones abandoned. Old and new programs must face the test of producing real results.

As the trends have changed, so also has the direction of the Department. Its major activities include curriculum planning, career education, drug use prevention, teacher evaluation, urban and conservation education, counseling and guidance services, and the year-round school. These activities specifically focus on improving educational quality and revitalizing elementary and high school programs.

Reforms under Superintendent Wilson Riles.   Wilson Riles, who was first elected in 1970, has insisted on these emphases. In late 1972, the Governor signed into law the Early Childhood Education Act, a bill for which Riles and the Department had worked hard. This Act provides for both restructuring and revitalizing primary education—a strong effort to upgrade teaching and programs in the early grades. In addition, the Department of Education itself has been reexamined and restructured to make it more pupil oriented, and to enable it to provide more effective assistance and leadership to the state's school districts.

Riles was reelected to a new term in the June 1974 primary. For his second term he stressed goals for high school curriculum. That program had to be revamped and new directions charted just as had been done for the elementary level. Riles advocated a shift from a high school program emphasizing college preparation to one teaching job-related skills, a learning situation more in tune with the world that faces many high school graduates. Riles also charged that the educational program was boring and stifling students, and his goal at both the elementary and secondary levels was to change that. To accomplish these educational goals in the 1970s, Riles' primary tactic was the continuing evaluation of the curriculum and programs. Accountability—the performance of a program—was the key element.[15]

Board of Equalization

In addition to the elected constitutional officers, the executive branch includes an important elected revenue board, the five-member Board of Equalization. Four of the members are elected to represent districts equal in population. The boundaries of each district are established by the state Legislature. The fifth member is the Controller.

The Board of Equalization is the state's major revenue agency. It administers several taxes, assesses utilities, and guides local officials in property taxation practices. The revenues administered by the Board—such as the sales, gasoline, cigarette, and alcoholic beverage taxes—represent the major portion of the state's income. (The sales tax alone brought in over $3 billion in 1974–75.)

The Board assesses public utilities and railroads throughout the state so that the taxation is uniformly assessed. It also encourages local property tax assessment practices that are the same for all counties by making sure that no county's assessment ratio of a property to its market value varies too much from the all-county average in the state. In addition, it trains tax assessors and their staffs for the entire state.

Other Boards and Commissions

A series of other boards and commissions exists within the executive branch, not directly under the Governor's authority. However, the Governor does influence the boards because he appoints their members. Because he is able to select persons whose ideas and beliefs are similar to his own, the Governor can significantly change the direction of a given board. Some appointments must be confirmed by the Senate, but a particular appointee is still likely to represent a position similar to that of the Governor who appointed him.

The number of appointments any Governor makes during his term is considerable; it may amount to several thousand. One estimate is that during former Governor Reagan's first term, he made almost 5,200 appointments. The job of drawing together names of potential appointees falls to the Governor's appointments secretary. He collects names from a wide variety of sources, and gathers information on these persons.

The Problem of Conflict of Interest

The task is to select for a particular board individuals who are willing to serve and who have the necessary interest and background to understand the concerns of the board, but who have no conflicts of interest through either their business or personal relationships. For some appointments, a major problem is that a member of a particular profession must be appointed to a board that oversees the work of that profession. This is the case with most boards regulating industry and professional activities, including the Boards of Pharmacy, Structural Pest Control, Optometry, Medical Examiners, Funeral Directors and Embalmers, Dental Examiners, Dry Cleaners, and the Contractors' State License Board. Others, like the State Water Resources Control Board, require that one have a particular background in order to be able to serve. To select a qualified individual who will not be charged later with a conflict of interest because of his own background or business relationships is sometimes a difficult task.

Some appointments are to important boards that meet regularly and possess a great deal of authority, others are to groups that meet just a few times a year and have only limited power. In either case, from the number of appointments constantly being made, it is easy to understand that the Governor may influence the thinking of a board no matter how independent its operation. Some of the more powerful bodies whose members are appointed include the Air Resources, State Water Resources Control, regional water quality control, and state and regional coastal zone boards, the State Energy Resources Conservation and Development Commission, the Regents of the University of California, and the Board of Education.[16]

The Board of Education and Board of Regents

Consider, for example, the importance of the Governor's appointments to the Board of Education. The Board member will have a direct say in establishing policies and regulations for the entire Department of Education. Thus, although the Superintendent of Public Instruction is an independent elected constitutional officer, he is in the peculiar position of having to carry out policies established by a Board made up of individuals selected by the Governor.

A similar example is the Board of Regents of the University of California. This Board was purposely established by the Constitution as a strong, independent agency, in an effort to shield it from political or religious pressure and influence. Once appointed by the Governor, a Regent serves for 12 years. Besides the 18 members appointed by the Governor, 7 other officials sit on the Board, including the Governor and Lieutenant Governor. In addition, the Regents may (if they choose) appoint one faculty member from a California college or university and one student member from a University of California campus. Before making his appointments, the Governor must consult a 12-member advisory committee. During his administration, Ronald Reagan made a determined effort to influence the decisions and thinking of the Board. In his opinion, the University needed more efficient management, better use of its resources, a greater interest in undergraduate teaching, and a firmer stand against student radicals. He attended Regents' meetings to voice his opinion and vote, something previous Governors had rarely done. As positions became vacant on the Board, Reagan also appointed individuals sympathetic to his views. In this manner, he was gradually able to force the Regents to consider his ideas.

Actually, a whole series of new problems was hitting higher education during this period. Many people felt there was a need to reevaluate the position and role of all institutions of higher education in California, including the state university and college system, community colleges, and the University of California. As in the elementary and secondary programs, many believe new goals are needed. For one thing, reevaluation is required because enrollment is expected to rise only slightly in the 1970s, and level out in the 1980s. At the same time, funding has become a major problem. Better coordination and planning are needed to meet the new problems of the 1970s. The entire idea, organization, and purpose of higher education is under review.

The Public Utilities Commission

Another body that has much influence in California affairs is the Public Utilities Commission, which is both a court and an administrative body. Subject to confirmation by the Senate, the Governor appoints five commissioners to serve six-year terms. This powerful body regulates the rates and services of privately owned utilities (such as gas, water, and electric utilities) and transportation companies (including railroads, buses, trucks, and airline companies). The Commission also establishes and enforces safety regulations, requires the filing of annual reports, and ensures that utilities operate at cost plus a profit not to exceed an established rate of return. To increase its rates, a regulated utility must demonstrate a need for the greater return. The Commission thus functions on behalf of public interest, ensuring that customers do not have to pay unreasonably high rates simply to increase utility profits.

A variety of other boards and commissions operate in California. While some, such as the Public Utilities Commission, are quite independent, all come under the influence of the Governor through his appointment powers. This means that while the powers of the executive branch are divided and the Governor maintains actual control over only a portion of the total, his influence is widely felt in other ways. The Governor's appointment powers, his budget-making duties, his lobbying measures, and his personal influence provide him with a great deal of power and authority.

Gubernatorial Campaigns

Because the position of Governor of California has a great deal of power and prestige, it is a highly prized and sought after office. In early 1973, Governor Reagan clearly declared he would not be a candidate for a third term. This left the Governor's race open to all who desired to run.

Campaign Financing

A mob of candidates quickly emerged, and the campaign was actually under way almost two years in advance of the November 1974 general election. One reason it began so early is that a well-run and adequately staffed California gubernatorial campaign probably costs over $3 million today. In 1970, Reagan spent $3 million in his winning campaign, while his financially strapped opponent spent just over $1 million. The big rush in early 1973 was to find contributors and supporters. Fund-raising dinners at $100 and up a plate mushroomed. Major candidates began planning primary campaigns costing over $1 million.

Money was available. The problem was that contributors wanted to be selective. One Orange County group of wealthy Republicans set out to interview potential Republican candidates with the intention of giving one individual major financial aid. Such tactics were criticized on the grounds that the groups were trying to play the role of kingmakers for the primary, destroying the open competition possible at the time because the incumbent was not in the race. But such action was hardly new to California. Both Republicans and Democrats have tried similar maneuvering before, only to be defeated.

It was quite clear, however, that a large amount of money was required to conduct an effective campaign—money for careful advance planning, a public relations firm to draw together a popular campaign to sell the candidate, and the use of expensive news media. Large contributors were needed. Special interest groups automatically became involved because not enough small contributors were going to participate to provide the huge sums involved.

The Field Narrows

By the latter half of 1973, the huge initial flock of candidates had thinned, and a few major contenders emerged. On the Republican side were State Controller Houston J. Flournoy and Lieutenant Governor Ed Reinecke. Because Reinecke's name was associated with political scandals on the national level, Flournoy turned out to be the more important of the two. A whole group of Democrats appeared but three were most publicized: Secretary of State Edmund G. (Jerry) Brown, Jr., San Francisco Mayor Joseph Alioto, and Speaker of the Assembly Bob Moretti. By the time of the June primary, eighteen Democrats, six Republicans, four Peace and Freedom candidates, and one American Independent candidate were still seeking their parties' nominations—some twenty-nine people in total! The two major contenders who emerged were Democrat Brown and Republican Flournoy.

The Brown–Flournoy Campaign

The fall campaign opened very traditionally on Labor Day in September 1974. During the days leading to the election on November 5, Brown (age 36) and Flournoy (age 45)—the youngest gubernatorial campaigners in years—made every effort to attract the interest of the California voter. They failed despite an intense effort to discuss issues and a massive input of campaign funds into media advertising to awaken that interest. Yet by the time election day came Brown and Flournoy had collected and spent $3 million to finance their primary and general election campaigns.

During the fall campaign, Brown maintained a wide lead in the polls over Flournoy, who had difficulty in communicating anything but a dull image. One major problem Flournoy never quite solved was how to divorce himself from the Reagan administration. In spite of his own philosophical differences with the incumbent Republican governor and his own opposition to many of Reagan's programs, he appeared too much a part of the past administration. Brown stressed that point, saying it was time to throw the rascals out. What was needed, he said, was a new spirit to breathe life and vigor into state operations. Brown was clearly the activist. Flournoy remained tied to those in office and to the programs of the outgoing administration.

Brown ran a very aggressive campaign. His advertising flooded California early during the fall campaign, and in a series of debates with Flournoy he assumed the aggressor role. Flournoy's campaign was slow in starting and suffered from a lack of money. Then in the final three weeks Flournoy made a determined effort to challenge Brown. He increased his media advertising tremendously, and by election day he was trailing Brown only slightly in the polls. Flournoy stressed his maturity, experience, and moderate viewpoint in contrast to what he said was Brown's more aggressive, shoot-from-the-hip, arrogant nature. Flournoy's campaign emphasized his long experience in government affairs as state Controller and legislator in contrast to Brown's brief experience as Secretary of State and a member of a local junior college board. Flournoy was characterized as someone who would cooperate and work well with legislators and state officials in solving problems, while Brown was labeled as an impatient, secretive person who would confront and dramatize issues.

Brown narrowly won the election. It was the closest gubernatorial election since 1906 and had the lowest voter turnout (63 percent) since 1946. Despite a general Democratic victory, Brown was not the major Democratic vote-getter that had been expected, and this came as a shock. Had the election come two or three days later, Flournoy could conceivably have won.

The major political question following the election was what Brown would be like as governor. After a great deal of analyzing and guessing, most political observers believed Californians would simply have to wait and see. Quiet, serious, reserved, cautious, ambitious, and sometimes hard-to-talk-to, the Governor-elect was a man whose course was difficult to anticipate. He had proclaimed the need for a new spirit in Sacramento. Clearly he was a part of the new politics of the 1970s, an activist more interested in listening to the voices of the broad base of citizens rather than the narrow one of special interests. But what new programs would he propose? In his campaign he had called for reform. He had suggested a one-house legislature, for example. In addition, he strongly had criticized the Reagan administration's ineffective efforts to end disorder and wasteful spending in government. He was interested in environmental protection and conservation and was a consumer advocate, promising to raise the director of the Department of Food and Agriculture to a cabinet level position. He had opposed the death penalty, called for liberalizing marijuana laws, and supported the right of public employees to strike. On the other hand, he was a strong advocate of law-and-order, for a hard, swift system of justice, and for a work instead of a welfare system. Some of his stands indicated that the conservationist and the consumer might well benefit from his appointments to various boards, such as the Public Utilities Commission and State Energy Commission.

However, many of his campaign statements would probably be of little value in determining the course of his administration. Several major tasks that had little to do with campaign issues faced the new Governor. One was to prevent the Democrats, who now controlled both the Legislature and the Governor's office, from fighting among themselves. What had to be put together in 1975 was a coalition that would provide the sound management and leadership Brown wanted. That would mean Brown would have to establish better legislative relations. During his campaign, he had accused legislators of being in the pockets of lobbyists and special interests. Now he would need legislative support to bring the new spirit to Sacramento. In addition, the budget surpluses of 1974–75 would no doubt vanish, and 1976 might well be a hard financial year. His promise to be frugal in budget matters, to be cautious in initiating new programs, to demand greater responsiveness from state government, and to listen to the broader public voice instead of special interests were most probably to be the keynotes of the new spirit, and were what California would most need in the second half of the 1970s.[17]

Review Questions

What are the basic duties of the Governor? How long is his term of office?

When is he elected? What are the qualifications to serve? Who determines the question of vacancy and who serves when a vacancy occurs?

Who serves in the cabinet?

What is the purpose of the cabinet?

What are the basic duties of the Department of Finance?

How flexible is budget planning? Why is budget flexibility an important issue?

What is an Agency? What does an Agency Secretary do? Who appoints Agency Secretaries?

What are some examples of departments and boards operating within an Agency? Who appoints the directors of the departments?

What two new executive departments appeared in 1973?

How have task forces been important? Give some examples of task forces and the results of their recommendations.

What is executive lobbying, and who does the lobbying?

What is meant by the statement that the constitutional officers divide the Governor's authority? How does their presence place restrictions on the Governor?

How many constitutional officers exist? What are the basic duties of each one? What two officers run their own separate departments? What are the qualifications to serve and when are they elected?

What is the name of the elected revenue board? What is its work?

How do the Governor's appointments to boards and commissions affect the work of those bodies? How does the Governor make his influence felt on these groups? What are some examples of these bodies?

Notes

1. Several brief illuminating articles including an interview with the Governor's Executive Secretary appear in the *California Journal* 1 (June, 1970): 151–157.

2. Some interesting comments by the Director of Finance as well as a discussion of the work of the department appear in the *California Journal* 1 (December, 1970): 334–341, 344.

3. This new department is discussed at length in the following article: "Massive New Department of Health, Reagan Administration's Most Ambitious Reorganization Plan, to Become Operational July 1st," *California Journal* 4 (April, 1973): 123–127.

4. An excellent overview of task force importance appears in "Governor's 'Legacy' Task Forces Seek Ways to Strengthen Local Government; Increase Public Safety, Cut State Taxes," *California Journal* 4 (January, 1973): 7–10. This article discusses further some of the points mentioned here. See also *California Journal* 4 (April, 1973): 133.

5. "Task Forces," 8–9, and *Los Angeles Times*, June 2, 1973; "Law-and-Order Report by Governor's Panel," *California Journal* 4 (September, 1973): 310–311.

6. Bruce Keppel, "Executive Agencies before the Legislature," *California Journal* 3 (December, 1972): 356–359. I have relied on this discussion for my remarks.

7. Ed Salzman, "A Sacramento Perspective," *California Journal* 4 (December, 1973): 398; Bruce Keppel, "Welfare Showdown: Reagan over a Barrel," *California Journal* 5 (January, 1974): 4.

8. Ed Salzman, "The State's New Stepping Stones to Higher Office," *California Journal* 4 (December, 1973): 415–416.

9. For a brief discussion of this office and an interview with Ed Reinecke see *California Journal* 2 (January, 1971): 4–7.

10. The *California Journal* 2 (February, 1971): 39–41, summarizes the duties of this office and has an interview with Edmund G. Brown, Jr.

11. For an interview with Flournoy and a description of the Controller's office see *California Journal* 3 (March, 1972): 86–89.

12. *Sacramento Bee*, May 19, 1973.

13. A short article on this office appears in the *California Journal* 2 (July–August, 1971): 208–209.

14. An interview with Evelle J. Younger and a description of the Department of Justice are in the *California Journal* 2 (April, 1971): 100–103, 116.

15. A brief interview with Wilson Riles may be found in the *California Journal* 3 (December, 1972): 360–362.

16. An interesting discussion of the problems that occur in making appointments appears in "Conflict of Interest Issue Eludes Easy Answers," *California Journal* 3 (March, 1972): 85.

17. "Front-Runner Jerry Brown—Republican Enemy Number One," *California Journal* 5 (February, 1974): 57–58. The August 1974 *California Journal* has three excellent articles on the gubernatorial campaign including an analysis of the differing philosophies of Flournoy and Brown. More on the campaign appears in the October 1974 *California Journal* article by Ed Salzman, "Looking Toward November," 5: 329–335; see also the article on the student vote in the same issue, 5: 336. Lou Cannon in the November 1974 *California Journal* has an interesting assessment of "The Reagan Years," 5: 360–366, as also does the *Los Angeles Times*, "Reagan's Quixotic Reign, 1967–74," September 29, 1974, Part V.

CHAPTER FIVE

THE LEGISLATURE

Overview

This chapter emphasizes the Legislature as a working body. The discussion stresses the legislative process and how it functions. Study the charts carefully because the material they include is not repeated in the chapter discussion, and they summarize many important formal details on the Legislature.

As you read this chapter, look for the answers to the following questions:

- How is the Legislature a process at work? How does the Legislature review the work of the other two government branches?
- How is legislative power divided and who holds it?
- How has legislative power been strengthened through 1966 and 1972 constitutional changes?
- What kinds of roles do the legislators have?
- Who are the important legislative officers? How do they control legislative activity?
- Why is the legislative committee the basic working unit of the Legislature? Which committees are the most important?
- What is the function of the legislative staff?
- What is a bill? How is it introduced? Who suggests ideas for legislation?
- What does the discussion of the Budget Bill reveal about the operation of the Legislature?
- How can a minority restrict legislative activity?
- How does lobbying affect a legislator?
- How does the discussion of the energy crisis show lobbyists at work? How does it reveal the role of the Legislature in solving problems?
- How can a legislator become trapped in a conflict of interest?
- What is the importance of the "fourth estate"?

These questions focus on the major themes of this chapter. If you are able to answer them and review the information summarized in the charts, you will have a good understanding of how the Legislature works.

Legislative Activity

The job of the California Legislature is to make laws to solve California's problems. Each year several thousand new proposals are submitted to the Legislature. Members must study them and enact those which they believe to be in the best interests of the state. On the surface, this may appear to be a relatively simple task, but it is actually quite involved.

Before a proposed law (called a *bill*) is enacted, it must be carefully studied, analyzed, and reviewed by legislators, the legislative staff, and legislative committees. Other individuals also may take an interest in a bill and offer their views on its strengths and weaknesses. These outsiders may include officials from state agencies, lobbyists or representatives of special groups, and individuals from the general public. Thus, a bill that is finally passed represents a great deal of work and energy spent in studying its meaning, purpose, and future effects on California.

The Legislative Process

More than anything else, the Legislature is actually a process at work. The major legislative function is the resolving of a variety of different interests into a single acceptable, workable solution. The Legislature is a "catchpool of ideas." What this means is that ideas from a variety of sources are actively gathered and thrust upon the lawmaker. His job, then, is to mold those ideas into legislation. The resulting law is really the work of many people who have bothered to press for or against the measure, and who have attempted to have it modified to fit their own interests. It is this study, negotiation, and blending of differing viewpoints that truly illustrates the work of individual legislators and the legislative process. This is what the Legislature as the state's chief lawmaking body is all about.[1]

Figure 18 lists some important points about the Legislature's members, their qualifications, and their terms of office.

The Work of the Legislature

The work of the Legislature involves activities of a broad nature. Through its staff and various committees, the Legislature conducts studies, collects information, and draws together recommendations on how to solve state problems. This work continues throughout the year, but is most intense during periods when the Legislature is in session. The subjects studied

Figure 18.   The California Legislature

	Assembly	Senate
Number of Members:	• 80	• 40
Term of Office:	• 2-year terms; all members elected every 2 years.	• Staggered 4-year terms; 20 senators elected every 2 years.

Both Houses:

Districts:
- Districts established on the basis of population in both houses.
- All Assembly districts have about the same population, and all Senate districts have about the same population.
- Each legislator (Assemblyman or Senator) represents a single district, and is elected by voting residents of that district.
- The Legislature reapportions these districts and determines district boundaries following the federal census taken each decade (1970, 1980, and so on).

Qualifications for Candidates:
- At least 18 years old.
- A resident of the district for 1 year.
- A resident of California for the 3 years preceding election.
- A citizen of the United States.

Time of elections:
- At general elections in November of even-numbered years (1976, 1978, and so on), on the first Tuesday after the first Monday.
- When vacancies occur, the Governor calls a special election to fill the vacancy.

include a wide variety of issues, such as law enforcement, court problems, education, taxation, and the environment.

As these issues are handled, the work of both executive officers and departments and court operations is being examined. In this way the Legislature evaluates the performance of the other two branches to discover how their operations can be improved, how new legislation may help, and how they may be forced to function more efficiently under existing laws. The review of the executive branch is most significant, for any

Legislature holds the executive accountable as to whether laws it has previously passed have been put into effect.

Legislative Power

The California Constitution clearly places the law making power of the state with the Legislature. This power is exercised by its two houses, the Senate and the Assembly. Yet despite this simple declaration, both the executive and judicial branches also hold some legislative powers.

Legislative Activities in the Executive Branch

The Governor has some important legislative duties. For instance, each year when he reports on the condition of the state, he can urge the Legislature to review his new ideas and plans. He may even choose to outline specific changes he would like made in the laws.

Budget Preparation. The Governor's most significant legislative responsibility is to prepare the state's budget for legislative review. The Legislature may revise some budget proposals and drop others, but it must enact a budget based on the one proposed by the Governor, and return it for his signature.

Item Veto and Veto. When the Governor receives an ordinary bill, he must accept or veto it *as a whole;* he cannot accept some portions and reject others. When he receives the budget from the Legislature, however, he has the right to exercise *item veto*—that is, he may reduce or cut out (but not increase) any appropriation in the budget, while still approving other parts and signing the budget as a whole. Through item veto, the Governor can change the budget to suit his own policies. The Governor may exercise this power on any bill appropriating funds. He can decrease or cut the appropriation while still signing the bill.

The Legislature may attempt to override a veto, though it has seldom done so successfully because that requires a two-thirds vote in both the Senate and the Assembly. Until 1974, no veto had been overriden since 1946. The Governor's veto powers are important because they permit him to challenge, reject, or change the work of the Legislature.

Special Sessions. The Governor also may call for a special session of the Legislature. When this occurs, he determines the subjects that are to be examined in the session. Thus, in several ways the executive branch is directly tied to legislative activity.

Legislative Activity in the Judicial Branch

The judiciary enters the legislative area by declaring laws or parts of laws unconstitutional. The court is also forced in some lawsuits to make decisions on how a law is to be applied, perhaps narrowing or broadening its effect.

Broadening Legislative Intent.   In the *Friends of Mammoth* case discussed previously, the California Supreme Court was forced to review the Environmental Quality Act. The issue was environmental impact reports, which the court decided had to be prepared for both public *and* private projects. The effect of the decision was to broaden the requirement, and the Legislature had to move quickly to establish the necessary methods for doing this. The result was that the Legislature added the court's decision to the law, and at the same time clarified the law.

Reapportionment.   The issue of reapportionment is another example of the courts' moving into the legislative area. Reapportionment of both legislative and congressional districts is a responsibility of the Legislature. Recently, however, the Legislature has found it difficult to develop a reapportionment plan acceptable to both the courts and the Governor. Objections to Legislature proposals have centered on two issues: first, the creation of oddly shaped districts to guarantee the election of certain types of legislators or the current officeholders (a technique known as gerrymandering) and, second, the existence of some districts containing far more people than others. The courts have demanded that more orderly boundaries be drawn and that district populations be more equal. In 1971, when the Legislature passed a reapportionment measure, the Governor vetoed it, claiming that many of the new districts had been gerrymandered. The California Supreme Court became involved at that point because the 1972 elections were approaching, and reapportionment had to be settled for those elections. After resolving the problem so that elections could be held, the court gave the Legislature another chance to solve the problem.

By 1973, the Legislature was still trying to meet court guidelines on reapportionment. At the same time, the court had created its own special group to draw up and submit a reapportionment proposal. The Governor announced once more that the Legislature's reapportionment measure was unacceptable, again because of gerrymandering, and he vetoed the measure. By mid-1973, it was quite evident that the reapportionment of both houses and the congressional districts would have to be left to the court, which finally adopted a reapportionment plan in November 1974.

The reason we have examined these legislative activities of the executive and judicial branches is that they illustrate that the division of government powers among the three branches is not clearly drawn. All three branches possess some legislative powers. As you learned in Chapter Four, a similar situation exists with executive power. A California Governor's use of executive power is limited by the existence of other elected officers, by a series of independent boards and commissions, and by great numbers of civil service employees who staff most of the positions in executive offices. Both the Governor and the Legislature have discovered from time to time that their power is limited as well as blurred. In the case of the Legislature and its power, this limitation is much more significant because until recently it functioned only on a part-time basis, unlike the other two branches, which operate continuously on a full-time basis. This has meant that it has been possible for them to expand their power at the expense of the Legislature.

Direct Legislation Activity: The Initiative and Referendum

California voters have also reserved some direct legislative powers for themselves. The initiative and referendum powers serve as an alternative method for voters to bring change in specific cases if the Legislature refuses to act. Californians have used the initiative extensively and have produced some remarkable changes.

For instance, as printed out in a previous discussion, in 1972 supporters of a proposal to protect the California coastline found the Legislature unwilling to pass legislation to establish that protection. They used the initiative statute process to place their proposal on the November 1972 general election ballot. California voters approved this idea, which created a series of coastal zone commissions and a single statewide commission to coordinate the protection of the coastline and to provide the planning for future more permanent regulation. Such use of the initiative process has made it a significant part of legislative power in California.

The initiative permits Californians to propose and pass their own laws and constitutional amendments; the referendum power gives them the opportunity to review acts already passed by the Legislature. Through the referendum process, most laws can be forced onto the ballot by circulating petitions asking that the law or a part of it be submitted to the voters within 90 days after its enactment or passage.

Strengthening Legislative Power

Because important pieces of legislative power are thus shared in California, the Legislature has worked hard to improve its own role. In the mid-1960s, for example, the Legislature made an effort to improve its constitutional position. Two basic aspects of the situation were dealt with: the problem of legislative pay and part-time legislative work, and the problem of legislative sessions. Legislators had been traditionally considered part-time workers and were paid accordingly. Legislative sessions were split into general sessions, which met every other year for 120 days, and budget sessions, which met on alternate years for 30 days. In these limited sessions, legislators found it hard if not impossible to deal adequately with California's growing and complex problems. A major difficulty was that general problems could be considered only every other year in the 120-day session, because only budget matters could be handled in the budget sessions.

1966 and 1972 Reforms

In 1966, California voters approved a far-reaching constitutional amendment that established annual, unlimited sessions in place of the biennial 120-day general session. It also proposed both a substantial pay increase and the possibility of additional increases on a regular basis.

The immediate effect of the 1966 amendment was to make the Legislature a continuously functioning body. The positions of Senator and Assemblyman became full-time occupations. The relationship of the Legislature towards the other two branches changed: it became more nearly equal. In 1972, voters approved another constitutional amendment that smoothed out the procedures and mechanics of meeting yearly, and established a two-year continuous session.[2] Figure 19 shows when legislative sessions are held now, in accordance with these recent amendments. Figure 20 shows the new legislative districts.

Figure 19.   Legislative Sessions

Regular Sessions:
- Are for a two-year period.
- Begin at noon on the first Monday in December of each even-numbered year (for example, 1974).
- End at midnight on November 30 of the following even-numbered year (for example, 1976).
- Are labeled 1973–74 Regular Session, 1975–76 Regular Session, and so on.

Special Sessions:
- Occur when the Governor causes the Legislature to assemble in special session.
- Consider what the Governor, by proclamation, determines will be studied; no other subjects may be considered.

Figure 20.   New Legislative Districts

Map Key
White numerals = Senate districts
Black numerals = Assembly districts
Broken line = division of each Senate district into two
            Assembly districts

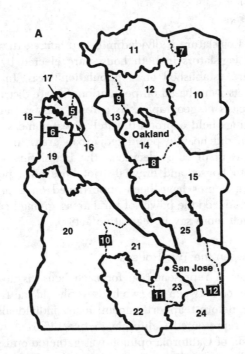

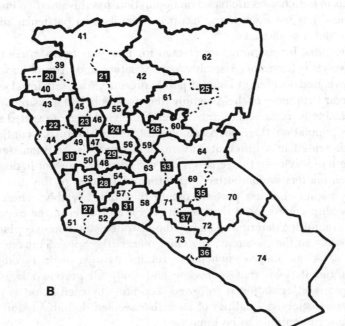

The Two Houses

The California Legislature is divided into two houses, the Senate and the Assembly. The legislators in both houses are elected by and represent districts that are established on a population basis. In the past, only Assembly districts were based on population; Senate districts were determined on the basis of geography. As a result, less populated areas and more rural settings held a proportionately greater measure of power in the Senate than did heavily populated urban areas. In the mid–1960s, however, as a result of court decisions, the Legislature was required to reapportion both houses and draw district lines on a population basis. Since 1966 both houses have been apportioned on a population basis. This action has reduced the power of rural areas, giving heavily populated urban areas much more say in legislative action.

Differences Between the Two Houses

Because the basis of representation for each house is now the same, is there any difference between the two houses? Should the Legislature have only one house? Before reapportionment, many individuals believed that the two houses represented California in two different ways, so that a good cross section of California opinion was gathered on issues. Now that districts in both houses are based on population, has this situation changed? The answer is no. Each house has preserved its own particular identity, despite the new districts.

Senators, for example, are elected for four-year terms in contrast to the two-year terms of Assemblymen. Senators and Assemblymen are, therefore, under different kinds of public pressure. Also, senatorial districts are larger than those of the Assembly (there are only half as many Senators as Assemblymen), so Senate districts tend to include a more varied section of the population than do Assembly districts. Californians continue to be represented in a different way in each house. In addition, seniority or length of service in the Senate is still considered important in determining such matters as committee appointments. Because of this, the Senate retains a somewhat less partisan nature than the Assembly, where party membership counts more than seniority. Furthermore, in the Senate the Rules Committee determines many administrative and housekeeping decisions, while in the Assembly, the chief officer (the Speaker) makes many major decisions. Lastly, each house retains its own distinct committee system and its own staff to review and study all proposed legislation. Each piece of legislation is reviewed separately by each house as before. Thus, the distinctive qualities of each that seemed desirable before reapportionment continue to be important.

The responsibilities and duties of both houses are actually almost the same. The only real difference is that the Senate confirms some appointments made by the Governor to various agencies, boards, and commissions, while the Assembly does not. Otherwise, the duties and powers of the houses are the same, as they were even when members were elected on two different bases.

A Unicameral Legislature?

During discussions of the virtues of single house (unicameral) legislature organization, it is usually mentioned that Nebraskans are very happy with their state government, the only unicameral legislature in the United States. In complex California, however, a unicameral body might not function so well. A comparison of the two states reveals many striking differences. California is urban, and has a diverse population with large, vital, and readily identifiable ethnic groups; it has almost 15 times more people, a larger number of poor, and many complex urban problems. If anything, Nebraska's population is remarkably *undiverse*. In that distinction may lie the key to why a single-house legislature is unlikely to be a good solution for California.[3]

Role of a Legislator

From what has been discussed already, you can understand that a legislator's job includes many activities and roles. One duty is to *develop and introduce legislation.* Ideas and suggestions for new laws originate from the legislator's own work and study, from his staff, from individuals in the district he represents, from his committee work, and from lobbyists for interest groups who know of his concern for specific issues or problems. Once a legislator has decided to use such an idea, he seeks the aid of the legislative staff (including his own office staff, the Legislative Counsel, and perhaps the Legislative Analyst) in preparing the necessary bill. In addition, lobbyists may be asked to supply suggestions, and executive branch departments also may help in preparing legislation. It is sometimes important to consult a variety of sources and learn their thinking about a proposed bill. This aids in drawing up laws acceptable to more people, and many times when a bill is controversial, consultation can help to diminish the opposition to it.

In addition to developing his own legislation, a legislator has the task of *reviewing and studying bills* introduced by others. Because he may have to vote on a particular bill, he will need to decide his own position on it, based on how it fits in with his own philosophy and his view of public needs or public interest, and how it affects his own district.

Individual senators and assemblymen also *work closely with the legislative committees* to which they are assigned. This means that they study the bills referred to these committees, attend committee hearings, participate in the discussion of proposed bills, and vote on whether to recommend a given measure for passage.

Through his work on committees, in organizing proposals to introduce as bills, in reading reports, and in consulting executive branch officials on problems, a legislator *keeps track of executive branch activities.*

Once legislation passes out of a committee it moves to the floor of the house for consideration. The legislator there *participates in those floor sessions,* perhaps becoming involved in debate on a measure, and, eventually voting for or against it.

A legislator also *maintains contact with the people of his district.* He may work with them to introduce legislation that will meet their district's needs, and he acts as their ombudsman. This means he serves as the person to whom the people of his district can turn when faced with problems in dealing with a state agency. He and his staff may spend a great deal of time in this role, and it is one of the most important and yet most overlooked aspects of a legislator's work. It is, however, a role that expands constantly as state government grows and as people more and more turn to their representatives for aid in handling problems. A legislator will also regularly *report to his district* on the activities of the Legislature. He may do so through newspaper articles, or speeches before various local groups, and/or he may distribute a mailer. This mailer probably will explain his views on certain issues. Some legislators have distributed mailers before an election explaining their positions for or against certain ballot propositions. For example, Senator Alan Short reported to the people in his district his strong opposition to Proposition 1 (Governor Reagan's tax initiative proposal discussed earlier) on the November 1973 ballot. Senator Short said he would vote no on Proposition 1 on election day, and he gave his reasons for opposing the initiative: he believed it to be a tax shift measure and not one of tax relief. He said it threatened to push more expenses on local governments and on local taxpayers, and he was concerned that it would undercut previous tax reform efforts. The accompanying illustration is a good example of the kind of *information mailer* that many legislators use to alert the voters in their districts to important issues.

Public Opinion *Versus* the Public Interest

Many people assume a legislator represents public opinion; he does not. In fact, his position on a given subject may be in conflict with the opinion of the voters in his district. *What a legislator should serve is the public*

Figure 21.   Candidates' Newsletters

SENATOR ALAN SHORT

...grams for the mentally retarded and the se- ...itizens. For ...rely physically handicaped within the framework of our

vestigate mittee, I throughout have been ... Hospitals w

s recei... ...r major concerns ...nergy crisis; and the ...

Capitol Report

Assemblyman, 40th District
Member, California State Legislature

ALEX GARCIA

...UAL RIGHTS AMENDMEN...

"The single most important reason women work is ...nomic necessity", states Anita Miller, Chairwoman of California Commission on the Status of Women. The ...mmission has found it especially shocking that the ...ning gap between men and women is actually in...asing.

Recently the commission received a grant of $288,000 ...om the Rockefeller Foundation to conduct a major im...act study on national conformance to the Equal Rights Amendment. At present the amendment needs ratifica...tion by five more states to become the 27th Amendment to the United States Constitution. The Equal Rights Amend...ment mandates that government at all levels — federal, state, and local — will conform laws to the principle of equality under the law for all people, regardless of sex.

This simple manda... changes in the la... will have profoun... such as the fami... tice system.

The State Le... current Resolutio... I co-authored AC... pointing powers ... crease the numb... missions to mor... in the voting ele...

"Conforma... of the Equal Ri... significant event

A REPORT TO THE PEOPLE

by
SENATOR MERVYN M. DYMALLY

on... l ...e... ... ...n ... r

GARCIA URGES POLITICAL REFORM

Democracy will not flourish in the dark. The public has a right to know exactly how its public servants are performing and how its interests are being served. With that thought in mind I have strongly urged my colleagues ...in the Legislature to join as early supporters of Proposi...-... line ballot. ...mon Cause and other con...-...onal spend-

Veterans t Assembly Bill 1 This bill i heritance tax pitalized, died vice in the Vi lowing: (1) C those militar ...it ni

VE...

STATE INCOME
TAX REFUNDS

The 1973 Session provided for disbursement of state surplus funds through income tax credits. Those filing their tax returns will receive this as a deduction from their tax liability predicated on the amount of taxable income reported. It has been brought to my attention that there is a large group of people who may be confused and may not receive this one-time benefit accruing to them. This is occasioned because through the use of the term "refund" many feel that a refund would only accrue to those who have made a payment.

Under the legislation that was enacted last year, renters for the first time get a tax credit and are entitled to a refund. This credit ranges from a minimum of $25 to a maximum of $45. Unless you file a state income tax return, you will not receive this refund or tax credit.

Many renters, particularly retired individuals, do not file income tax returns because they do not have sufficient income. However, this year I suggest you contact the State Franchise Tax office nearest to you and inquire as to your eligibility for the renters tax credit. The office in Stockton is located at 31 East Channel Street, Room 244; and the office in Sacramento is located at 920 23rd Street. If you did not take this credit when you filed, you can file an amended return.

ey or RI M, ist pla c ely Si e p sen er i ne fate.

...eastern California, that have suffer... frankly, I had assumed, and I think everyon he Legislature did, that because of the drastic ...ic changes in the districts, the Court would election in every district as they did in 1966. ately, such was not the case. I have met with ...nal experts and public officials thro... t, and it is my consid... ...y will be with... ...rs. This is one of two are. legal act...

interest. His knowledge of public needs—not of public opinion—should guide his votes. Public opinion can change quickly, and may be based on incorrect information, ignorance, or prejudice.

In most situations, of course, the question of public interest versus public opinion presents no real problem, because there may be no public reaction to a given issue. Most Californians probably know very little about the bills under study. On some bills, however, a great deal of publicity and resultant pressure may develop.

In 1973, many legislators found themselves caught up in this kind of situation on the death penalty issue. California laws providing for the death penalty had been struck down by the courts, but much public pressure had developed to reestablish that penalty. First, in November 1972, voters approved an initiative amendment that established a new base for laws permitting the use of the death penalty for some crimes. The Legislature then came under intense pressure to pass legislation to that effect. By the late summer of 1973, many legislators were caught between demands for the reestablishment of capital punishment, and their own beliefs that such legislation should not be passed. Some legislators accepted the force of public opinion and voted for the law over their own serious personal objections. As a result, in September 1973, the Legislature passed and the Governor signed a bill reestablishing the death penalty provision for some crimes.

As he attempts to serve the public interest, a legislator may also face a second kind of pressure, that of special interest groups, who will try to persuade him that what they want is truly in the public interest. Thus, a legislator may often find it hard to perform his role of determining the real public need and holding out against the pressure of public opinion that he feels is incorrect, or of special interests.

Some have argued that because of these pressures on legislators, perhaps a cover of secrecy needs to be maintained over some decision making and voting. In this way a legislator will be freer to vote in the public interest, shielded somewhat from intense outside pressures. Critics, of course, have charged that any secrecy is dangerous, and rather tends to allow special interests to bring even more pressure to bear on representatives. Openness, they say, is the real cure.

Lastly, legislators also must *maintain an active role in their political party.* This means attending party meetings and participating in a whole series of party activities.

Summary of Legislator's Responsibilities

A legislator has a series of roles or responsibilities. He develops legislation and introduces bills. He reviews and studies other legislation before the

Legislature. He has many committee assignments to perform. He keeps watch over executive branch activities. He participates in debates and votes on legislation in floor sessions. He maintains contact with the people of his district by making reports, giving talks, and acting as ombudsman. He serves the public interest and determines what is best for public needs despite the pressures of public opinion or special interest lobbying. He retains an active interest in party work and participates in party activities.[4]

Because the roles of a legislator are many and varied, and because together these responsibilities comprise a very heavy workload, legislators carry out their work with the aid of a rather important legislative staff. This staff supports not only the work of individual legislators but also the work of legislative committees and the Legislature in general. Legislators' efficiency in accomplishing their variety of roles depends in large measure upon the work of this staff.

Organization of the Legislature

Officers

Two types of officers are present in each house. One type, chosen from the membership of the Legislature, is the key leader, who carries on the major work of supervising legislative activity. The second type is not from the membership of the Legislature but employed to do much of the ordinary administrative work that enables the Legislature to run smoothly. The tasks of this group include supervising minute-taking, acting as parliamentarian, supervising the printing of bills, and maintaining order. Figure 22 shows these principal legislative officers, some of their duties, and how and by whom they are chosen.

Figure 22.   Officers of the Legislature

ASSEMBLY	*SENATE*
Officers elected from Assembly membership:	Lieutenant Governor • Is president and presiding officer, under the terms of the Constitution.
Speaker and Speaker pro Tempore • Both members of political party holding a majority of seats in the Assembly. • Speaker pro Tempore fills in when Speaker is absent.	Officer elected from Senate membership: President pro Tempore • Elected by Senate from the membership of the majority party.

Assistant Speaker pro Tempore
- Appointed by Speaker
- Performs duties of Speaker pro Tempore in his absence as they relate to presiding over the daily sessions of the Assembly.

Majority Floor Leader
- Appointed by Speaker, from majority party.
- Is Speaker's personal representative on Assembly floor.
- Duty is to help speed up Assembly's work and make it progress as smoothly as possible.

Minority Floor Leader
- Selected by minority caucus.
- Represents political party holding a minority of seats in the Assembly.

Officers selected from outside:

Chief Clerk, Sergeant at Arms, and *Chaplain*
- Elected by Assembly members.

Minute Clerk
- Appointed by Chief Clerk.

- The major officer in the Senate.
- Shares the administration of the Senate with the Rules Committee.

Officers selected from outside:

Secretary of the Senate and *Sergeant at Arms*
- Elected by Senate members.

Assistant Secretary, Minute Clerk, and *Chaplain*
- Appointed by Senate Rules Committee.

The Power of the Speaker

The most important and most powerful officers are, of course, those selected from the membership of the Legislature. In the Assembly, the key figure is the Speaker, whose powers were greatly expanded in the 1960s. Today, the Speaker controls much of the Assembly's operation. Thus, if the Speaker is solidly against a bill, its supporters usually have the choice of either seeing it fail or of modifying it to gain his acceptance. A Speaker will not and does not control every piece of legislation, but if he chooses to commit himself and take a stand on a particular bill, his position will probably prevail.

Committee Appointments. The Speaker can have and maintain such a vital role by carefully using the powers assigned to his office. For example, he appoints the chairman of the all-important and powerful Rules Committee, although its members are elected by the Assembly as a whole. The Speaker determines all committee chairmen and vice chairmen, and any subcommittee established by a committee to help in its work must be approved by the Speaker. He has the power to appoint, as a majority of any committee, legislators who are in agreement with his views on particular subjects. Thus, committees of the Assembly many times reflect the interests and feelings of the Speaker, and because of this, he can sway the outcome of much legislation.

Other Powers. In addition to his role in determining the makeup of committees, the Speaker schedules committee meetings and refers bills to committees, both actions that can influence the outcome of legislation. For example, if a committee meeting to consider a particular bill is held at odd hours or in conflict with other meetings, that bill's fate can be significantly affected. And while the referral power may seem slight, it is highly important. When a bill is introduced for consideration, the Speaker is to assign it to the "proper" committee for study. He is the one, though, who determines which committee is proper. For example, a bill dealing with agricultural labor might be studied by the Agriculture Committee or the Labor Relations Committee. One committee might react more favorably to legislation favoring growers, while the other might be likely to support a strong measure in favor of farm workers. Thus, the decision as to which committee receives the measure for study has everything to do with the kind of bill that eventually will be presented to the Assembly for final vote. Lastly, because the Speaker conducts the actual floor sessions of the Assembly, he can by his use of parliamentary rules and procedures influence the vote on legislation. These are some of the more significant powers of the Speaker. Still more exist. In total, they can enable the Speaker not only to manage the Assembly, but at times to run it as a virtual dictator.

In mid-1974 the Assembly selected Leo T. McCarthy as its new Speaker. McCarthy set out on a reform course changing committee chairmen and indicating more changes were to come. He anticipated altering the committee structure to reduce the number of committees, to provide for more active sub-committees, and to expand the power of the Rules Committee, allowing it some of the responsibilities held by the Speaker, such as determining the assignment of bills to committees.

President Pro Tempore

The Senate's mode of operation is somewhat different from that of the Assembly. The Constitution establishes the Lieutenant Governor as President of the Senate. Even though his duties are chiefly ceremonial and he has almost no power, he does preside over Senate meetings.

In reality, the major officer in the Senate is the President pro Tempore. Like the Assembly's Speaker he is elected by the Senate from the majority party. Unlike the Speaker, his powers are restricted because he must share the administration of the Senate with the Senate's Rules Committee, of which he is the chairman. Other Rules Committee members are elected by the Senate. Thus, his power over Senate activities depends in large measure on how much he can sway and control the other members of the Rules Committee, which makes Senate committee appointments, determines committee chairmen, and refers bills to committees for study. The powers of the President pro Tempore are controlled not only by the Rules Committee, but also by the fact that seniority or length of time in the Senate counts much in determining membership on committees and chairmen.[5]

Committees: How They Function

Legislative committees are absolutely vital to the legislative operation because they must handle the tremendous work load placed upon the Senate and Assembly. Thousands of measures (over 7,000 in the two-year 1973–74 session) are presented each year for study, and each house relies on its committees to examine them. Committees, therefore, are the basic working units of the Legislature.

Some 17 standing committees in the Senate and 20 in the Assembly investigate proposed legislation. In addition to these regular standing committees, subcommittees are at work, and at various times special investigating committees are formed to consider particular subjects.

Committee Membership.   As pointed out previously, memberships on committees and chairmen are determined by the Speaker and the Senate Rules Committee. The total membership on a committee varies. In the Senate, the smallest committee has five members and the largest thirteen. Each legislator is assigned to several committees. Senators, for example, serve on about four different committees. In the Senate, membership is based quite closely on seniority, while in the Assembly, the Speaker is more concerned with party membership in making appointments to committees and chairmanships. Figures 23 and 24 show the committees for the 1973–74 legislative session. As a committee studies a bill, it is actually carrying on several activities, each supported by the legislative staff. Each committee, for example, is assigned a consultant to aid in its review of bills.

In addition, committees can call upon the Legislative Analyst and Legislative Counsel.

Figure 23.   Senate Committees (1974)

- Agriculture and Water Resources
- Business and Professions
- Education
- Elections and Reapportionment
- Finance
- Governmental Organization
- Health and Welfare
- Industrial Relations
- Insurance and Financial Institutions
- Judiciary
- Local Government
- Natural Resources and Wildlife
- Public Employment and Retirement
- Public Utilities and Corporations
- Revenue and Taxation
- Rules
- Transportation

Figure 24.   Assembly Committees (1974)

- Agriculture
- Criminal Justice
- Education
- Elections and Reapportionment
- Energy and Diminishing Materials
- Finance, Insurance and Commerce
- Governmental Organization
- Health
- Human Resources
- Intergovernmental Relations
- Judiciary
- Labor Relations
- Local Government
- Public Employees and Retirement
- Resources and Land Use
- Revenue and Taxation
- Rules
- Transportation
- Urban Development and Housing
- Ways and Means

Steps in Studying a Bill

What activities make up the review of a bill? Factual information on a proposal is assembled. Necessary research studies are performed. The Legislative Analyst estimates the bill's financial impact. The Legislative Counsel is asked to consider the legal impact of the proposal as it affects existing laws, and he may be asked to decide if the proposal is constitutional. Committee hearings are held to collect testimony from the legislator who introduced the bill, and from executive officials, specially interested groups, and the general public. As this work unfolds, existing and related programs are reviewed. Executive branch activity in the area of study may be examined. New suggestions may be offered as amendments to change the original bill.

Committee Action.   Once this entire process is completed, the committee takes action on the revised bill. Each committee member's vote is recorded in an open public meeting. Figure 25 indicates the choice of actions.

Figure 25.   Committee Actions

In voting on a bill, a committee may
- Recommend passage.
- Recommend approval with amendments.
- Recommend amendments and re-referral to the committee for additional study.
- Reject it. (This means it is probably dead for that session.)
- Retain it in committee for study (and thus usually let it die there).

Several points are important to keep in mind as you think about final committee action. First, some bills are simply never considered by committees, are never reviewed, and, therefore, never come to a vote. So many bills are introduced that there is not enough time to study all of them. Second, if a bill is approved and sent by the committee to the floor of the house for action, it will probably pass that house. A bill rarely fails to pass, once a committee recommends it. Third, once a committee rejects a bill, it is usually dead for that session. Committee action, therefore, means life or death for most legislation.

Committees of Special Importance

Committee on Rules.   Some legislative committees have special influence and are particularly important. We have already looked at the Rules

Committees in both houses as examples. The Assembly Committee on Rules acts as the executive committee of the Assembly, though its duties relate more to the administration of the Assembly than to reviewing proposed legislation. The Senate Committee on Rules is also charged with general responsibility for the administrative functioning of the Senate, but it is more powerful than the Assembly Committee. Its duties include referring bills to Senate committees for hearings, appointing members to committees, and receiving nominations from the Governor for boards, commissions, and agencies that must be approved by the Senate. Figure 26 summarizes some of the general tasks performed by the two Rules Committees.

Figure 26.   Committees on Rules

Assembly Committee on Rules
- Appoints employees of the Assembly and reviews their work.
- Makes studies and recommendations to improve the procedures of the Assembly and its committees.
- Secures the services of outside public or private agencies when needed.
- Assists the work of the other Assembly committees.
- Supports the work of individual members of the Assembly.
- Provides needed secretarial assistance to committees and members.
- Controls the spending of funds appropriated to support the Assembly.
- Continues its work around the year even if the Legislature is not meeting.

Senate Committee on Rules
- Carries out all the above duties on behalf of the Senate, and in addition:
  - Determines the membership of Senate committees.
  - Appoints chairmen and vice chairmen of committees.
  - Refers bills to committees for study.
  - Reviews for recommendation nominations sent by the Governor to the Senate for confirmation.

Fiscal Committees.   The fiscal or finance committees of the two houses are also of major significance. In the Assembly, this body is known as the Ways and Means Committee; in the Senate, it is referred to as the Finance Committee. The Ways and Means Committee is the most powerful in the Assembly. In either house, any bill that requires any appropriation of funds or affects state revenue and spending must come before these committees for study. Such a bill is first referred to the standing committee that deals with the topics it covers, and then is passed along to the fiscal committee for consideration. Because these committees review so many bills, they hold a powerful influence over the total legislative program.

Conference Committees. Another important body is the conference committee. A conference committee is formed when a bill dealing with a specific matter has passed both houses but is in two different forms—an Assembly version and a Senate version. If, for example, an Assembly bill is amended in the Senate and the Assembly refuses to accept the Senate amendments, a conference committee is established. Three of its six members are appointed by the Speaker, the other three by the Senate Committee on Rules. This committee attempts to work out the differences between the two versions. If it fails, a second committee is appointed. Up to three committees may be approved for any one bill.

The Question of Secrecy

In the past, legislators often made key decisions in closed committee meetings, with the votes of individual legislators unrecorded. To a remarkable degree, that has changed. Voting must now take place in open meetings, and the vote of each committee member must be recorded. However, the problem of secrecy still remains. Much of the vital decision-making process has continued to be done in informal or closed meetings. The last committee to have a formal, closed meeting was the all-important Senate–Assembly conference committee that worked on the final version of the 1973 budget. Following the approval of the budget, the two houses voted to open to the public the joint committee's sessions.

The 1973 Reforms. The 1973 efforts to end closed meetings marked a significant step towards opening up for public hearing some of the key meetings where major decisions are made. In June 1974, California voters approved a legislative constitutional amendment confirming this trend. The amendment specifically required both the sessions of each house and the committee meetings of each to be public. The only exceptions to this have to be provided for by a law or concurrent resolution approved by a two-thirds vote of each house. Thus, only in carefully defined situations can meetings be closed.

Disadvantages of Open Meetings. Political reformers have welcomed this trend toward openness and believe more is in order, but problems do exist with this open setting. It is true that "wheeling and dealing" should decrease, and that compromises will be observed and recorded in the open sessions. But informal pre-hearing meetings still will take place, and much decision making goes on in such off-the-record gatherings. Furthermore, the Governor's office will continue to hold meetings to try to influence members and work out problems on current legislation in the privacy of the Governor's office.

Open roll call voting also may make it almost impossible to kill legislation that favors special interests. Such special interests as church groups, teachers' organizations, and state employee groups will probably gain greater influence as a result of recorded voting. They will be able to identify opposition votes more easily and thus mount more effective campaigns to win the votes needed for legislation in which they are interested. These same groups also can more readily identify their legislative friends and enemies at election time. Therefore, on the one hand, the public will know when legislators remain firm against special interest pressure and can support their legislators for not weakening. On the other hand, special interest groups will know which campaigns to contribute to and which legislators to support most actively.

Legislative Staff

Almost 1,900 people aid California legislators in fulfilling their responsibilities. Of that total number, over 700 make up a full-time professional staff. The staff includes not only those attached to a legislator's own office, but also those assigned to committees and other offices, such as that of the Legislative Counsel or Legislative Analyst. Together this staff provides an individual legislator with the legal information, fiscal or financial reviews, background information, and research work that he needs to accomplish his job.

The existence of a large, full-time legislative staff has expanded the influence and importance of the Legislature over the last few years. Most of the staff growth has come recently, but some offices have existed for several years: the Legislative Counsel, the Legislative Analyst, and the Auditor General.[6]

Legislative Counsel

The position of Legislative Counsel was established in 1913 to provide the Legislature with legal services. These include aiding any member in drawing up legislation, providing summaries of bills that show changes to be made in the existing law, assisting state agencies in preparing measures to be introduced, and supplying members of the Legislature with legal opinions on matters under study by them (such as whether or not a bill is constitutional).

Auditor General

The office of the Auditor General, along with the Joint Legislative Audit Committee, was created in 1955 and includes a staff of about 50. The committee, which is made up of members from both houses, appoints the Auditor General and establishes the policies of his office. One of the Auditor General's chief duties is to provide the Legislature with an independent audit to determine whether or not appropriations to the executive branch have been used properly and are in line with the Legislature's intended purpose. These audits also help both the legislative and executive branches in deciding good financial policy for the state.

The fact that the Legislature carries out its own audit to see how funds are being spent serves as a check both on executive authority and on the effectiveness of the work of the Department of Finance. It makes the legislative branch a more independent unit, because the Legislature does not have to rely solely on the word of the executive branch that funds have been properly used.

The work of the Auditor General has tended to be noncontroversial, and has not attracted much attention. This fact in itself became significant; some legislators wanted the Auditor General's reports to move away from their purely bookkeeping nature to include a review of state programs on the basis of their effectiveness and efficiency as well. Pressures of this kind mounted until in 1972, the person who had served as Auditor General since the creation of the office was fired. In the fall of 1973, a new Auditor General was hired to accomplish these broader tasks, with the help of an increased staff and budget. The reports that the new office began to release showed a new emphasis on examining the performance of a department or agency. The reports were more critical in tone, and stressed performance and the elimination of inefficiency to save the state money.[7]

Legislative Analyst

A major problem in legislative work is that the budget submitted to the Legislature for approval is mainly the work of the Department of Finance, whose Director is the Governor's chief advisor on financial matters. The budget therefore expresses the Governor's approach to state government, and is intended to carry out his policies. Once the budget is presented, the Legislature must determine its merits, decide whether or not it needs changing, and whether programs should be added or eliminated. This is a hard task because the Legislature must accomplish the review without the resources that the executive branch departments used to make up the budget.

In 1941, believing that more careful reviews of the budget should be undertaken, the Legislature established the Joint Legislative Budget

Committee. This body, which is made up of 14 members, seven each from the Senate and the Assembly, reviews the budget and the revenues and expenditures of the state, as well as the organization and operation of the various state agencies. The purpose is to reduce the cost of state government and obtain greater efficiency and economy. To fully carry out these goals, this committee appoints the Legislative Analyst.

The Analyst's Budget Review. The Analyst's major task is to analyze in detail each item of appropriation suggested in the Governor's Budget, or in any appropriation legislation, and then make specific recommendations to the committee. This review also supplies the Legislature the base for advancing its own programs and making changes in state appropriations. The Analyst's study of the Governor's Budget is important not only to the joint committee, but also to the Senate Finance Committee and the Assembly Ways and Means Committee, which review the budget as well. The information gathered by the Analyst's office is available to all legislative committees and all members of the Legislature.

In his examination of state spending, the Analyst may suggest important changes. In 1967, for example, the Legislative Analyst's office urged a new approach to state supervision of health care. From this suggestion came studies that produced legislation to create the Department of Health, which began operations in July 1973. The Analyst's office, upon request, also puts together proposals or programs for a particular legislator, though its overall purpose is to serve the Legislature as a whole.

The Analyst's work, like that of the Auditor General, has resulted in expanded reputation and power for the legislative branch, because it has provided the Legislature with independent information. The Analyst's functions and those of the Auditor General have greatly aided the Legislature in effectively evaluating the budget and proposed programs, gaining a much better accounting of state revenues and spending, and determining if that spending is done as the Legislature intended.[8]

Assembly's Office of Research

The Assembly also maintains its own Office of Research to provide additional studies beyond what the Legislative Counsel, Analyst, or Auditor General supply. Its professional staff and files aid both Assembly committees and individual members of the Assembly in making in-depth studies of major legislative problems.

The Office of Research also keeps a record of research projects under way by Assembly committees or other public or private research agencies on topics that are under consideration by the Legislature.

Legislative Bills

Bills, Amendments, and Resolutions

In any legislative session, several thousand bills are introduced for consideration. A *bill* may intend one or all of several actions: it may be to establish a new law, or change or remove an existing law. *Amendments* to the California Constitution are also considered by the Legislature; they are reviewed and treated in the same manner that bills are.

Distinct from bills and constitutional amendments are *resolutions*. Several types of resolutions exist. A *joint resolution* relates to matters affecting the federal government, such as ratifying a proposed amendment to the federal Constitution. *Concurrent resolutions* relate to subjects concerning both the Assembly and the Senate, such as the Joint Rules of the Senate and Assembly, which establish broad guidelines for the work of the Legislature. (They set up, for example, the calendar to be followed for a legislative session.) *House resolutions* relate only to matters affecting a single house, such as rules for the Assembly or Senate. Joint and concurrent resolutions are considered by both houses, house resolutions only by a single house. In general, resolutions are examined in a speedier and more simplified manner than are bills or constitutional amendments.

Sources of Bills

When a legislator introduces and sponsors a particular bill, he may be presenting either a measure that he himself has developed, or one that has been suggested to him from any of a wide variety of sources. For example, the Governor makes some recommendations for legislation. His staff makes the necessary studies and draws together proposals. Or the staff may work with outside committees, such as the task forces the Governor has appointed on law enforcement, tax reduction, and transportation. Once the suggestions and ideas are drawn together, the Governor's staff finds legislators to introduce the resultant bill. In addition, executive branch agencies and departments suggest legislation, which is then introduced by an individual legislator. For instance, in 1973 the Secretary of Health and Welfare and the Governor were actively pressing for basic changes in the structure of the Health and Welfare Agency. The Secretary wanted to combine departments and rearrange some functions of the Agency. Both he and the Governor were pushing for legislative approval of their idea.

Constitutional officers also may draw up proposals and search out sponsors for them. For example, Attorney General Evelle Younger was interested in having a number of changes made in existing laws to improve law enforcement and court proceedings. His office conducted the needed

---

Figure 27. Sources of Bills

- Legislators
- Legislative committees
- Legislative staff
- Governor
- Executive branch agencies and departments
- Constitutional officers
- Special interest groups

---

studies and research and prepared the recommendations. Then he and his staff looked for legislators to introduce their ideas as bills. Before Controller Houston Flournoy was first elected in 1966, he had campaigned on the need to reform the selection procedures of inheritance tax appraisers in order to prevent abuse of their powers. After his election, Flournoy actively urged legislators to alter the system, and while he did not convince them of the need for all the change he wanted, he did succeed in obtaining partial reform.

Proposals also may come from the legislative committees or staff. In the process of a committee's investigation of particular subjects, it may determine that legislation is needed and may urge its initiation. By the same procedure the staff may draw together proposals based upon its work in support of committee research or in response to a legislator's request that a bill be prepared on a given subject. The Legislative Analyst is especially important in suggesting legislation because his work focuses on the Budget Bill.

In addition, suggestions for bills come from sources outside the government. Individuals representing industry, corporations, environmentalist groups, church groups, teacher organizations, labor unions, or other special interest groups encourage legislators to introduce legislation that these groups believe to be important. The representatives of these various interests will also gather information and ideas to help in drafting the bill.

Introducing a Bill

Before a bill is introduced into either the Assembly or Senate, it must be reviewed by the Legislative Counsel. The Counsel prepares a digest of the bill, briefly stating the changes to be made in existing law. Once the digest is made, the bill is ready to be introduced. Now the bill, signed by its author and any coauthor, is presented along with the digest to the Secretary of the Senate by Senators or to the Chief Clerk of the

Assembly by members of the Assembly. The bill is then assigned a number (Senate Bills are designated SB 1, 2, and so on, and Assembly Bills AB 1, 2, and so on), and its title is read before the house for the first time. It is printed, and then referred to the appropriate committee for review. Except for the Budget Bill, no bill may be heard or acted upon by any committee until it has been in print for 30 days. Some 17 standing committees in the Senate and 20 in the Assembly investigate the legislation introduced. In addition to these regular standing committees, subcommittees are at work, and at various times special investigating committees are formed to consider particular subjects.

The Budget Bill

One of the most complicated and difficult bills the Legislature must study and enact is the Budget Bill. This bill is introduced each year, and the Legislature spends several months reviewing the suggested appropriations. Even though it is complicated and has several characteristics different from other bills, an examination of the process used in reviewing and studying the Budget Bill will illustrate much about how the Legislature operates. A good understanding of the discussion that follows will provide a basic knowledge of how the legislative process works and how a bill is handled.[9]

Introduction of the Budget Bill

As discussed earlier, once the Governor and his cabinet have outlined budget policies and the Department of Finance has drawn up a budget reflecting those policies, the Governor submits his Budget together with his Budget Message to the Legislature. The Governor's Budget is then introduced as an appropriation bill, that is, the Budget Bill, in both the Senate and Assembly by the chairman of the fiscal (finance) committees of each house. This Budget Bill is referred to the Senate Finance Committee and the Assembly Ways and Means Committee for their study. Thus, in 1973 Senator Randolph Collier introduced the Budget Bill as SB 80 and Assemblyman Willie L. Brown, Jr., introduced it as AB 110. Each man was chairman of the fiscal committee in his particular house.

The Work of the Legislative Analyst

The work of these two committees is assisted by the Legislative Analyst, who reviews the budget for the Legislature. As the Department of Finance draws together the Governor's Budget, it forwards confidential reports to the Analyst, enabling his office to prepare its studies in advance. Then, when the Governor sends his Budget to the Legislature, the Analyst can present his report. His findings and recommendations are prepared and presented as the *Analysis of the Budget Bill*. Even though this *Analysis* is for the use of the whole Legislature, it is especially designed for the Senate Finance and the Assembly Ways and Means Committees, which must investigate the Bill and hold hearings on it. In 1973, the Governor forwarded his Budget and Budget Message to the Legislature on January 18, and on February 5 the Legislative Analyst presented his 955-page analysis to the Legislature.

In the *Analysis* the Legislative Analyst reports on each item of appropriation with a recommendation. He may agree with the Governor's request or he may recommend the item be increased or decreased or even eliminated altogether. On the other hand, the Analyst may suggest changes in a particular area to bring greater efficiency and to cut expenses. It was this type of suggestion on health care services in 1967 that brought the studies recommending a new Department of Health. One of the chief purposes of the Office of the Legislative Analyst is to discover better and more efficient procedures in order to reduce costs and to avoid unnecessary or overlapping programs.

Analyst's 1973 Comments.   The 1973 *Analysis* of Governor Ronald Reagan's Budget was rather unique. Reagan had built for himself the image of a conservative tightwad in budgetary matters. Previous budgets had hit hard in greatly limiting funds for education, welfare, health care services, and state employee benefits. However, the recommended 1973 budget was, at that time, the largest ever sent to the Legislature. In contrast to the 1972 budget of $7.7 billion, the proposed 1973–74 budget was over $9.2 billion.

The Legislative Analyst's review of the budget suggested that the Governor was overgenerous in his requests for money. One example was in the area of higher education, especially the pay increases recommended for State University and College faculty and the budget's building construction suggestions for all levels of higher education. The Analyst also was critical of the budget for the Department of Social Welfare. The recommended increased funding for this Department was questioned because its responsibilities were being redefined and limited.

In addition to these comments, the *Analysis* made several recommendations. For instance, the report suggested legislation was needed to remove the administration of welfare from county control, a recommendation that has been made repeatedly since 1968. The Analyst's office has maintained consistently that state administration would end duplication of effort and be a more effective and more economical method of controlling welfare.

Significance of the Analyst's Work.   The *Analysis* of the 1973 Governor's Budget illustrates well the function of the Analyst's office and the importance of the legislative staff. Because of this *Analysis,* the Legislature had before it an evaluation of the budget based on facts. It also had a critical review of budget items with specific recommendations, and suggestions on how to improve state operations, increase state efficiency, and cut costs.

Committee Work and Hearings

Once the Budget Bill has been introduced and the *Analysis* completed, the fiscal committees of each house are ready to study the proposed budget. The examination of the Budget Bill extends over several months, but, according to the Constitution, the Legislature must pass budget legislation by June 15 and send it to the Governor for his signature so that the budget will be ready for the start of the fiscal year beginning July 1. If the Legislature fails to meet the June 15 deadline, it must continue meeting until the Budget Bill is passed.

In the months before the budget is put into final form and sent to the floor of each house for a vote, several actions may occur. For example, the Governor may change his recommendations. In 1973, for instance, the Reagan administration increased its requests by over $48 million—from $9.25 billion to $9.3 billion. The fiscal committees may also change the recommended expenditures. In 1973, the problem of federal funding, discussed earlier, was one serious consideration. To cover programs cut from federal funds, some provision was made to increase state allocations for those programs. Such problems are not only studied by the staff and the legislators, but also are reviewed in the committees' hearings.

Hearing Process.   As the committees carry on their work, hearings are held to gather information on various appropriation items. At these hearings several points of view are heard. For example, the Department of Finance may attend the hearings to justify and defend its recommendations. The Office of the Legislative Analyst will be present to note and defend its remarks made in the *Analysis.* The particular state department or board affected by the appropriation also will attend to discuss the purpose and need of the appropriation and, in effect, provide expert testimony. In addition, members of the public as well as representatives of interested groups may attend and discuss their opinions.

Expenses of the Legislature

Some budget items receive a great deal of attention; others do not. One very sensitive budget section involves the expenses of the Legislature itself.

The 1973 *Analysis* included little about this section. For some time, critics of legislative expenses have maintained that the rise in legislative costs is unchecked—that neither the Legislative Analyst nor the Governor carefully examines nor comments on legislative spending. In fact, these same critics believe that the Legislature does not investigate the spending activities of the Governor's office, either.

Most of the money to operate the Legislature is appropriated to three funds. Each house has its own fund and controls it through its own Rules Committee. A joint fund for both houses is under the supervision of the Joint Rules Committee. Two basic problems exist with these funds; first, no readily available public records are kept of expenditures, and, second, knowledge of how these funds are to be spent and of the purposes for which they are used is hard to uncover. Yet these funds are used to pay the expenses of the California Legislature, including the legislative staff (such as the Auditor General and Legislative Analyst), the work of legislative committees, and contracts for all special studies and projects. In 1973, over $33 million was appropriated to these three funds.

Some critics have attacked not only the lack of accountability as to how the money in these three funds is spent, but also some of the procedures used in determining actual budget item figures.

Budget Conference Committee Work

In late May 1973, the Senate Finance Committee brought its budget study to a close. The Assembly Ways and Means Committee had finished its work earlier, so that version of the budget had been brought to the Assembly and approved. The Assembly bill then had been sent on to the Senate. Now the Senate Finance committee amended the Assembly's bill to conform to the Senate's lower budget figures, and the Senate approved it. When the bill was returned in this amended form to the Assembly, it refused to agree to the Senate changes, and a budget conference committee was formed to work out the differences. As is normal in such action, this joint conference committee consisted of three members of the Assembly and three Senators.

The Importance of Committee Work.   Budget conference committee activity is unusually important. Because a two-thirds vote is required to pass the Budget Bill, a great deal of bargaining and compromising must go on in committee until acceptable figures are reached. Unless problems are successfully resolved there, the necessary two-thirds majority may not be obtained in each house. That can result in major battles on the floor of each house and additional committee work.

The 1973 Closed Meetings.   The 1973 meetings of this conference commit-tee reflected an older legislative pattern: its meetings were closed. In fact, the original Senate budget version had been voted on by the Senate Finance Committee in secret, and an embarrassed chairman had to recall his committee to have a public vote recorded! Now in the closed joint conference committee meeting the budget was put into final form. The committee reported to the Legislature a final $9.4 billion budget, which it had determined in secret. This budget was approved by the Senate and the Assembly. These secret meetings in which the real budget for California was determined were typical of much of the decision making that has occurred in the Legislature.

Private sessions also marked the spring 1973 efforts to find a reappor-tionment solution. Public votes were taken on this important issue, but the real decisions were made in closed meetings. Despite efforts to require open voting and force public sessions, informal meetings will continue to be an important part of committee work.

The 1974 budget conference committee activity furnished some marked contrast to the 1973 work. The Legislature had previously deter-mined that this conference committee work would be open and, for the first time, those meetings were reported by the news media.

Presenting the Bill to the Governor

The Governor can only approve or reject an ordinary bill, but he has the privilege of *item veto* on appropriations bills such as the budget. Thus, when Governor Reagan received the 1973 Budget Bill, he reduced appro-priations by vetoing or reducing budget items by $78 million before signing it. The resulting $9.3 billion budget was still the largest in California history and the largest of any state in the country. (The 1974 budget topped $10 billion and was surpassed only by the budgets of New York State and the federal government.)

The Budget Bill Process

This examination of the Budget Bill of 1973 shows the legislative process in operation. Some features of the study of the Budget Bill are special to it, but nevertheless, its progress through the Legislature illustrates the workings of the Senate and the Assembly. Ordinary bills must wait 30 days before being heard or acted upon by a committee; work on the Budget Bill begins almost with its introduction. In considering the Budget Bill, the whole legislative staff, but especially the Legislative Analyst, is important in the investigation of the budget items. Second, the legislative committee is also of vital importance in the examination of the budget.

Committee activity and hearings reveal an openness and flexibility

Figure 28.   Deadlines for Bills

- In the *second year* of a regular session, no bill may be passed by either house on or after September 1 except for (1) statutes calling elections, setting taxes, and making appropriations; (2) urgency statutes; (3) bills passed after being vetoed by the Governor.
- In the *second year* of a session no bill may be sent to the Governor after November 15.
- The *Budget Bill* must be passed by June 15 each year.
- *Carryover of bills:* In the two-year regular session, bills introduced the first year may be *carried over* into the second year *if* they are passed by the house in which they were introduced by January 30 of the second year of the session.

Figure 29.   Governor's Action on Bills

Presenting Bills to the Governor:
- Bills passed by the Legislature are presented to the Governor for signature.
- They become law if he signs them or if he does not return them within 12 days.
- In the second year of a regular session, any bill passed by the Legislature before September 1 and in the possession of the Governor by or on September 1 becomes a statute unless returned by the Governor before September 30.

The Governor's Veto Power:
- A Governor vetoes a bill by refusing to sign it and returning it to the house where it was first introduced; he must send along a statement of his objections.
- On appropriations bills, the Governor has the right to item veto portions of any appropriation while still approving other portions of the bill; this means he may cut out an item or reduce the funding for an item, but he cannot increase the amount appropriated; for item vetoes he must inform the Legislature of his reasons for the veto.

Overriding a Veto:
- The Legislature has 60 working days in which to reconsider bills vetoed or items vetoed by the Governor; if each house reconsiders the bill and passes it by a two-thirds vote within that time, it becomes law.

Figure 30. When Statutes (Laws) Take Effect

- Statutes passed at a *regular session* go into effect on the January 1 following a 90-day waiting period after the law has been enacted.
- Statutes passed at *special sessions* go into effect on the 91st day after the end of the special session at which the bill was passed.
- Statutes calling *elections,* providing for *taxes,* or providing *appropriations* go into effect immediately upon their passage.
- *Urgency statutes* take effect immediately upon their passage. (Urgency statutes are laws necessary for the immediate preservation of public peace, health, or safety. They require a two-thirds vote in both houses.)
- Initiative statutes, initiative constitutional amendments, and referendum acts take effect the day after they are approved by the voters.

---

that is very special to the California legislative process. The emphasis is on gathering and welcoming a flow of information from a variety of sources. Both independent staff reports and testimony from non-legislative sources play important roles at committee hearings. Other legislatures in the United States are not as open to this free flow of outside testimony and reports. On the other hand, while official closed meetings are now a thing of the past, informal private meetings remain. And those unreported and unrecorded meetings are where much of the real legislative work is accomplished through bargaining and compromise.

Third, the use of a joint conference committee to solve the differences between the Senate and Assembly versions of the Budget Bill illustrates the normal use of such conference committees. They meet to work out the differences of bills that have proceeded through both houses, and then report the results to each house, which may accept the new negotiated version of the bill.

Fourth, perhaps what the budget-making process really shows is how various opinions must be harmonized if any work is to result. This is not only true of differences among legislators themselves but also of the relationship between the Legislature and executive branch officials and departments. Their requests for funding of state programs place upon the Legislature the responsibility of determining if a program is worthy of appropriations, if funds exist to support it—and if money is not available, what other state operation may be cut back or eliminated in order to finance it. This process makes the Legislature an active, functioning branch of state government. The major legislative function is still the resolving of a variety of interests into a single whole. Selecting programs that are workable and will be of greatest benefit to the state is a difficult task. In the end, some important programs may sometimes be overlooked, and unimportant ones supported but the total result should be a basically sound, intelligent, and workable package.

Fifth, the fact that the budget is sent to the Governor for his signature reveals that legislative power does not go unchecked. Through the item veto of the Budget Bill, a Governor can force the state's budget to reflect his philosophy and policies, regardless of how important the Legislature may consider the programs funded in the budget. The Governor has the last say; vetoes are rarely overridden.

The Usual Bill Process

The ordinary bill is introduced only in *one* house, but it proceeds through committee study, hearings, and action just as the Budget Bill does. If the bill is recommended by the committee that has it under study, and if it proceeds through normal legislative procedures of a second and third reading on the floor of the house and is passed, it is then sent to the other house for review. There it is referred to a committee for study, hearings, and action. If the second house changes the original bill, and the house where it was introduced does not approve the change, a joint conference committee is formed to work out the differences. If this committee succeeds in ironing out the differences and the revised bill is passed by both houses, it is presented to the Governor.

The Public Interest and Minority Control

The public interest or majority view should most often prevail in the legislative process. Many times it does not. The reason is that certain rules allow special interests or minority views to block legislative proceedings by skillfully using certain legislative voting requirements that are written into the California Constitution.

Voting Requirements Help
Special Interest Groups

For example, most California taxes that directly affect the ordinary citizen (such as the gas, sales, or income tax) may be raised by a majority vote of the Legislature, but a two-thirds vote is required to raise the tax rates for banks, corporations, and insurance companies. In addition, a two-thirds vote is required for other important legislative decisions: (1) to pass the Budget Bill; (2) to override a Governor's veto; (3) to pass a bill containing an urgency clause allowing it to take effect at once; (4) to submit a constitutional amendment to voters; and (5) to submit a bond issue to the voters.

These constitutional voting requirements have allowed groups to slow down the legislative process or bend it to their will. This has happened with attempts to raise taxes on banks and corporations, as well as on efforts to pass Budget Bills. In 1973 and 1974, unusual harmony prevailed over the Legislature in the development, study, and final approval of the Budget Bill. In other years, however, the budget debate has been marked by hostility and bitterness. In fact, budget passage has often been delayed because a minority of legislators has refused to join the majority and make up the two-thirds vote needed to pass the Budget Bill.

Furthermore, because a two-thirds vote is required to override a Governor's veto, no Legislature was able to do so from 1946 until 1974. In January 1974, a veto by Governor Ronald Reagan was overridden, but in seven years he had successfully vetoed about 1,000 other bills. The vetoes of Governor Goodwin J. Knight (1953–58) and Governor Edmund G. (Pat) Brown, Sr. (1959–66) were never challenged. Governor Earl Warren was the one overridden in 1946. Even though a majority (over half) of the Legislature may want to override the Governor's veto, they cannot do so unless a full two-thirds of the members feel that way.

Thus, a relatively small number of individuals can block passage of significant pieces of legislation. If special groups apply heavy pressure to legislators and convince them to withhold their vote, a few individuals can obstruct the will of the majority. For example, to block a measure requiring a two-thirds vote in the Senate, only 14 Senators need to be persuaded to vote no, even though 26 are in favor of the measure.

Committee System Encourages Control by Minority

It is also possible to handicap the legislative process through other means. The committee system itself encourages control or at least management by some individuals. As we said earlier, the Speaker and Senate Rules Committee control the appointment of legislators to committees, designate to which committee a bill is to be referred for study, determine the extent and time of legislative hearings on a bill, and decide the time and circumstances of the final vote on a bill on the floor of the Legislature. All these heavily influence the fate of any measure. If it is referred to a hostile committee or a vote on it is scheduled at the least favorable time, these actions may kill it without giving it a chance to survive.

Of course, to alter the regulations so that majority rule can prevail in all instances needs the approval of the minority, so such change is practically impossible to achieve. For example, to reduce any of the constitutional two-thirds vote requirements requires a constitutional amendment, and such amendments need the two-thirds approval of the Legislature. To use the alternative method of the initiative process takes a well-organized, well-financed drive, first to circulate petitions, and then to persuade voters to approve the issue.

Minority Interests

Who is the minority that uses these tools? It may be a particular political party, a special interest group, or a group representing a specific geographic area. For example, a minority may represent a particular issue of interest to northern Californians, such as that of water resources, and may use these constitutional devices to control legislation. On the other hand, a special interest group may block legislative action on matters that adversely affect its interests. These self-interest groups tend to represent portions of the more well-to-do, more expressive, middle-class element of society. These are the groups that can organize and finance an effective effort to influence the government process.

The real danger, of course, is that when powerful special interest groups are combined, they form a privileged majority, and the less privileged elements—the poor, welfare recipients, elderly, and racial minorities—have little if any influence on the government process.[10]

Lobbying and Special Interests

Special interest groups exert pressure through lobbying. Lobbyists direct their efforts toward all kinds of government officials, agencies, and boards, but their primary focus is on the Legislature.

Lobbyists and their Legislative Work

The Governor, of course, is the chief lobbyist, but executive agencies and departments also maintain a series of legislative coordinators to help push through bills. In addition, legislators are pressured by representatives of all sorts of special groups, corporations, and industries, and various local governments and their divisions.

Lobbyists discuss their clients' views and needs not only with legislators but with legislative staff as well. They may attend committee hearings, watch the roll calls, and testify about bills concerning their clients. Many times, lobbyists present useful and needed information and ideas about the future impact of proposed legislation. It is easy to understand why they are sometimes labeled the *Third House* of the Legislature.

Several hundred lobbyists are present at each legislative session. Many register formally, but others are not required to do so because they are volunteers, not professionals, or because they represent church organizations. When the number of registered lobbyists is added to those who do not register, the total is indeed impressive.

Pressure Methods

Legislators feel the pressure of lobbyists in various ways. At office meetings, over informal lunches and dinners, or through his staff, a legislator may become acquainted with a particular special interest's view. Lobbyists used to be allowed to contribute directly to campaigns, but the 1974 Political Reform Act ended that. However, the groups a lobbyist represents may still participate in campaigns to support friends and defeat enemies.

California teachers are a good example of a group that has decided to expand its lobbying activities to include campaign work. In spring 1973, the California Teachers' Association (CTA) began a major drive to encourage its members to become involved in local school board elections. The purpose was to support board members friendly to teachers' interests and to defeat those who were hostile. When the election results were in, in many cases the teacher-backed candidates had won, and the CTA felt this proved teachers had a direct political influence and were willing now to use it to support or defeat legislators who refused to listen to the CTA position. The most significant point about this development was that the teachers' group was not only willing to lobby in the Legislature, but also to campaign actively when necessary to support or defeat legislators. By using this campaign threat, the CTA hoped to hold more influence over legislators.[11]

The Energy Crisis as an Example of Legislative Activity

One of the most interesting results of lobbying activity happens when different special interest groups and their lobbyists oppose one another. The energy crisis was a major issue in 1973 that brought environmental groups and industry and corporation interests into direct conflict. As Californians became aware of the energy crisis, they were flooded with suggestions on how to meet it. Most of these recommendations came from three groups: the Legislature, environmental groups, and the power utilities.

It became almost immediately apparent that the Legislature rather than the executive branch was going to lead in uncovering solutions to energy problems. In 1972, the Assembly Committee on Planning and Land Use had already asked the Rand Corporation in Santa Monica to study the problem of energy planning. The Rand study was presented to a subcommittee in the fall of 1972, and the subcommittee began to explore what role state government ought to have in setting energy policy for California. The Rand report was friendly to the environmentalist viewpoint in two of its basic conclusions: first, that the demand for energy must be reduced and held down and, second, that new power generation facilities must not harm the environment.

Environmentalists and Energy Controls.   After the subcommittee released this report, environmentalist groups began strong lobbying in favor of setting limits on energy use and on protecting California from a sudden effort to build as many power plants as possible to meet future energy demands. One major lobbying effort was under the direction of the rather powerful Planning and Conservation League, which represented a series of environmental groups. The League pushed to create a commission to take action in several ways: supervise the planning to meet future energy needs, support research into new means of generating electricity (such as using solar energy and geothermal—underground—steam energy), set rates for the use of energy, and control the approval of new power plant sites.

In response to the Rand report and environmentalist suggestions, five power utilities in California hired the Stanford Research Institute (SRI) to prepare a study of California energy needs. SRI criticized many of the Rand suggestions, and predicted that energy needs would be met without restricting the use of electricity, through the building of nuclear power generating plants. SRI saw little hope of relying on the use of solar and geothermal energy sources for some time to come. In its opinion, the reduction of energy demands was a poor suggestion because the state's economy relied on expanding energy use. The task was to make energy use more efficient and to begin building more nuclear power plants to meet the expanding need.

Subcommittee Work.   To resolve these different viewpoints, the subcommittee on energy planning began to gather further information. First, it sent out a questionnaire to public utilities, environmental groups, and government agencies asking their opinions on what the state might do to create energy policy. Second, it held a series of hearings where each side presented its views. When the hearings were finished and the subcommittee and legislative staff had reviewed the information collected, Assemblyman Charles Warren, who was chairman of the subcommittee, introduced a bill into the Assembly.

Bills Introduced.   The Warren bill intended several things. It created the energy commission the environmentalists wanted in order to fund research, prepare plans to meet future energy needs, create policies to hold down the need for energy use, and authorize the building of new power plants once they had been safely sited. While the bill did not do as much as environmentalists wanted, it did propose that the state take a much more active role in energy planning. Other bills were also introduced into the Legislature, including one by Senator Alfred Alquist which focused on the problem of siting power plants. As we said in Chapter Two, Warren and Alquist eventually sponsored the successful bill that passed the Legislature and was signed by the Governor in May 1974. Thus, the Legislature, not the executive, acted to find a solution to the energy problem.

Legislative Process Illustrated

This description of the response to the energy crisis demonstrates the Legislature's role in determining state policy—in this case an energy policy, and the creation of a commission to carry out that policy. The work of the Assembly Committee on Planning and Land Use shows how legislative committees rely on staff reports, widely distributed questionnaires, and outside studies (such as the Rand report) to gather information to help in drawing up legislation. Furthermore, the work of environmental lobbies and those representing the public utilities and industry show that when a controversial issue arises, lobbying can reveal a wide variety of conflicting views about that issue, providing legislators with a variety of opinions on the probable effect that legislation will have if enacted.

The energy crisis reveals special interests actively at work lobbying for their own interest and attempting to say their interest is the public interest. Environmentalists believed they were protecting the environment for the public's welfare. The utilities believed they were serving the needs of California by working to meet expanding energy demands for personal and industrial needs. It remained the Legislature's task to define the public interest and to protect it from special interests.[12]

Conflict of Interest

Several difficult problems face a legislator in carrying out his responsibilities. One major problem is that of potential conflict of interest. In Chapter Three, basic causes for conflicts of interest developing among public officeholders were discussed. Legislators' association with lobbyists or their business holdings may cause conflicts. If a legislator becomes too close to special interests, he may look after their needs more than the public interest and public needs. Campaign contributions are only one of the major sources of conflicts.

Legislator Using Office for Gain

How a person uses the office of Assemblyman or Senator also may create conflict of interest problems. Almost no conflict of interest arises because of actual bribes, but a legislator may become overcommitted to the interests of a certain group or groups. He may discover that when he is in contact with state officers or others on legislative matters, those individuals may try to help him because they believe that will aid them in getting future favorable bills introduced. A legislator who is a lawyer has particular problems if his clients deal with state offices. He may be tempted to use his office to aid his clients by pressuring state agencies to give in to client demands. Or he may write bills that benefit his clients. To avoid such problems, many legislators have found it best to restrict or abandon their legal practice. This tendency has been strengthened by the fact that legislators are now considered to be full-time workers, but some legislators still try to carry on both their legislative duties and outside occupations.[13]

Critics also have charged that some legislators actively use their staff to improve their image with the voters. And of course, an officeholder often uses his staff to convince the public that he is doing a good job, during reelection periods.

One of the most serious aspects of this problem involves the use of mailings to voters at public expense. Some legislators have used mailings only according to the strict purposes allowed by the law to provide important information to the people of their districts, but others have abused the privilege and sent out publicly financed mailings that are, in effect, campaign literature.

The Fourth Estate

Much of the credibility of the Legislature depends upon the mass media, or the fourth estate, as it has come to be known. The importance of the mass media has grown in recent years primarily because of television. Many legislators—and really all state officers and agencies—have found it wise to develop a good image and use the media for their own advancement. Legislative as well as executive offices issue countless reports and news releases discussing the importance of their work, hoping that reporters for newspapers, radio, and television will use the material.

The Problem of What Is News

The media often object to being the tool of this type of public relations effort. Their task is, after all, to uncover news stories, not to inflate the images of particular legislators. Reporting the news of the Legislature is not always an easy assignment. Many stories are released to the media, but legislative sources do not usually volunteer controversial news. Therefore, a reporter must first uncover a story and then ask questions about it. This type of reporting is especially valuable in determining the activities of the Rules Committees and the expenditures of the Legislature's funds.

Many times legislators see the media as hostile because they do not publish the carefully written releases, but choose instead to report other news—controversial expenditures from legislative funds, or controversial individuals or agencies hired to carry out research for the Legislature. For instance, in 1973, in an effort to aid the development of nonpolluting cars, the Assembly paid to have steam cars built. Some reporters found this an unusual expense and wanted to know if any friends of legislators had benefited from the experiment.

The Importance of Media to Legislators

News releases that are carefully written and present an ideal image are most valuable for any legislator when published in the newspapers of his district. On the other hand, news media relations may be tense as newsmen attempt to report uncomfortable stories about legislative personalities or actions, or attempt to record the workings of floor sessions and committee hearings. But because a good press image is important, many legislators make strong efforts to develop friendly relations with newsmen.[14] This helps in getting good news reported and may aid at times in avoiding the reporting of unfavorable stories.

The Hazards of Being a Legislator

The ten hazards described in Figure 31 are intended to be humorous, but they do sum up the problems facing a legislator as he carries on his day-to-day business. Those hazards may develop slowly and almost unnoticed; a legislator must remain alert to them and avoid them. If he does, the legislative process will stay alive and healthy, and the legislative branch will be strong and effective in meeting and solving California's problems.

Review Questions

What legislative power is held by each of the following: the Governor, the courts, and the people?

What is the importance of making the Legislature a year-round body, and the job of legislator a full-time job?

What are the legislator's eight roles?

What does a committee do? What do the Rules Committees do? What are the names of the two fiscal committees, and what do they do?

How does the legislative staff aid the Legislature, particularly in relation to the executive branch?

Figure 31.   The Vocational Hazards of a Legislator
Senator Albert S. Rodda

Several years ago I began a list, now consisting of ten items, which I regarded as a legislator's vocational hazards.* All legislators are exposed to these hazards. Some succumb; others resist.

First:	Obesity
	(chicken, mashed potatoes, and peas circuit)
Second:	Egocentricity
	(fatheadedness)
Third:	The Third House
	(lobbyists and special interest groups)
Fourth:	The Fourth Estate
	(the mass media)
Fifth:	A Fifth
	(gin, bourbon, scotch, vodka, etc.)
Sixth:	Erosion of Basic Commitment
	(politics of expediency)
Seventh:	Image Makers
	(Madison Avenue P. R. men)
Eighth:	La Femme
	(redhead, blonde, brunette, etc.)
Ninth:	Political Cronyism
Tenth:	Cardiac Arrest

*These are listed in the order of their development, not by any priority. You are privileged to arrange your own priorities. I do think that the tenth should come last; it seems a potential concomitant of the first nine!

What are the functions of the Legislative Counsel, Legislative Analyst, and Auditor General?

How does a bill proceed through the Legislature?

How is the legislative process characterized by both openness and secrecy?

How do two-thirds vote requirements influence legislative action?

What is the role of the lobbyist?

What is "conflict of interest"?

How does the "fourth estate" affect legislators?

Notes

1. Former Speaker Jess Unruh is the one who described the Legislature as a "catchpool of ideas." See Donald G. Herzberg and Jess Unruh, *Essays on the State Legislative Process* (New York: Holt, Rinehart and Winston, 1970), pp. 29–30. This small book is a collection of essays that covers a number of topics mentioned in this chapter and has some interesting observations on the California Legislature.

2. "The Two-Year Session: Success or Failure?" *California Journal* 5 (January, 1974): 11–12.

3. Dennis J. Opatrny, "Nebraska's Unicameral—Would It Work Here?" *California Journal* 5 (May, 1974): 167–168.

4. Richard W. Gable and Alexander Cloner, "The California Legislator: A Study of the Job and Factors Related to Compensation," prepared for the Constitutional Revision Commission acting under the Joint Committee on Legislative Organization, California Legislature, January, 1965, pp. 18–20.

5. The *California Journal* conducted interviews with Speaker Bob Moretti and President pro Tempore James Mills in which both men discussed their duties. For Moretti, see *California Journal* 2 (May, 1971): 128–129, 132, and for Mills, see 2 (March, 1971): 66–68. More material on the Senate is presented in Alvin D. Sokolow, "The State Senate in Transition: A Study of the Declining Importance of Seniority in the Upper House," *California Journal* 2 (October, 1971): 280–283. When Moretti revealed his intention to run for Governor, there was a scramble to succeed him. Leo McCarthy won. See Jerry Burns, "The Fall and Rise of San Francisco: the Race to Succeed Moretti," *California Journal* 4 (November, 1973): 365–369; Ed Salzman, "The Constant Quest for the Speakership," *California Journal* 5 (March, 1974): 95–96; "How McCarthy Won the Speakership," *California Journal* 5 (July, 1974): 245; "The New McCarthyism," *California Journal* 5 (August, 1974): 269–270.

6. "Legislative Staff of 1500 Provides Administrative Support and Professional Aid to Lawmakers," *California Journal* 2 (April, 1971): 96–99, 114–115. This article discusses the general importance of the staff and some more specific points about the staff members who are discussed in the rest of this section; Dennis Dorch, "Legislature's $25 Million Staff," *California Journal* 5 (August, 1974): 271–273. The article is a more critical review of the staff.

7. Bruce Keppel, "Coming on Strong—State's New Auditor General," *California Journal* 5 (May, 1974): 163–164.

8. An interesting interview with Legislative Analyst A. Alan Post appears in the *California Journal* 1 (May, 1970): 138–139; "How the Legislative Analyst Operates," *California Journal* 4 (October, 1973): 341.

9. The *California Journal* 2 (February, 1971): 36–37, has an interview with Assemblyman Willie L. Brown, Jr., on the budget process. Brown has been chairman of the Assembly Ways and Means Committee.

10. Albert S. Rodda, "On Majority Rule," a talk given on March 24, 1969; "What on Earth Are We Doing about Getting Good Government?" a talk given on January 30, 1967; "Essential Meanings of Democracy," *California Elementary Administrator* 31 (May–June, 1968): 25–26.

11. The *California Journal* has published a series of interesting and very informative articles on lobbying including "Lobbyist Campaign Contributions," 1 (September, 1970): 262–263; Laura Magnani, "University and College Students Seek to Establish an Effective Presence in Sacramento," 2 (November, 1971): 306–308; "Lobbying the Legislature: Facts, Friendship, Favors, and Flim-Flam," 3 (August, 1972): 212–216; "The Lobbyists the Public Pays: One of Every Ten Advocates Represents Local Government," 3 (October, 1972): 292–296; "Ambitious Plans to Tighten Control of Lobbying Must Counter Legislature's Disinterest in Doing So," 4 (April, 1973): 128–129; Richard Rodda, "Death of Artie Samish: Lobbyist's Legacy Lives," 5 (March, 1974): 100; Chris Wahle, "Who Are Sacramento's Most Influential Lobbyists?" 5 (September, 1974): 293–295.

12. See Chapter Two, note 9.

13. Herzberg and Unruh, pp. 79–86; *Los Angeles Times*, June 22, 1973.

14. "Political Profile of Capitol Press Corps," *California Journal* 5 (February, 1974): 55–56; Ed Salzman, "A Personal Perspective," *California Journal* 5 (May, 1974): 146.

CHAPTER SIX

THE JUDICIARY

Overview

This chapter reviews two basic matters. First, it describes the structure and functioning of the California Court System. You will need to know about the four levels of the court system, the relationship among these levels, and the important role of the Judicial Council and two Commissions. Second, the chapter discusses a few of the controversial issues that recently have been brought to the courts for decision. You should understand how the judicial branch is as involved in solving California's problems as the other two branches you already have studied.

California courts have a strong influence on the lives of Californians, and this influence has broadened in recent years. Courts have made decisions affecting the environment, educational financing, the death penalty, and the very sensitive political issue of the reapportionment of legislative and congressional districts. Even Californians who were not directly affected reacted to these decisions because of their controversial nature. For instance, when the court abolished the death penalty it *directly* affected the lives of only 106 people, but it awakened the emotional feelings of many others who either strongly opposed the decision or who supported it and were grateful it had finally come.

The judicial process must deal with a wide variety of cases. Ordinary criminal cases (such as those for murder, burglary, and so on) and civil cases (such as those dealing with contracts or divorces) may become highly significant when the courts' decisions overturn existing practices and require new approaches. This, of course, is exactly what occurred with the decisions on the death penalty and on educational financing.

Two Court Systems

Two court systems exist in the United States: state and federal. Both systems have specific responsibilities and functions. Each is separate from the other.

The state courts handle most of the court cases. For almost all cases state courts follow state law, but in some instances they must turn to federal court decisions and federal law. Federal courts, on the other hand, follow federal law except when they are handling a case involving state law, when they must follow state court decisions and state law. As Figure 32 shows, appeal is possible from state courts to the federal Supreme Court, if a federal issue is involved in the case. Appeals are most often made from the California Supreme Court rather than from the lower courts.

Figure 32.   Appeal in the Two-Court System of the United States

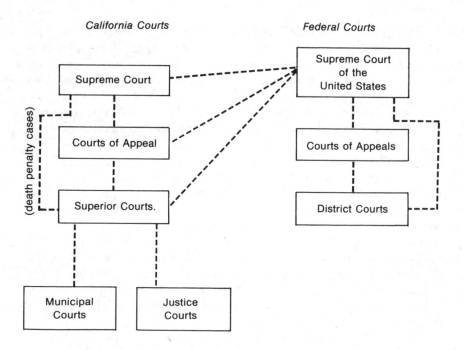

Judicial Power

The California Constitution places the judicial power of the state in four levels of courts: (1) Supreme Court, (2) Courts of Appeal, (3) Superior Courts, and (4) Municipal and Justice Courts (which are known as inferior courts). All of these except the Justice Courts are *courts of record*—that is, they retain permanent records of proceedings.

Even though the Constitution clearly assigns judicial power to the courts, other bodies operate to handle narrowly defined matters in judicial-like proceedings. For example, the five-member Public Utilities Commission, which establishes the rates to be charged for the transportation of passengers and freight by all transportation companies in the state, has a judicial character. Other similar bodies are the Board of Equalization, the Fair Employment Practices Commission, and the Industrial Accident Commission. The Fair Political Practices Commission is another excellent example. Voters approved its creation as part of the Political Reform Act of 1974; it began functioning in February 1975. The Commission's hearings and responsibilities in enforcing the Reform Act give it a definite judicial appearance.

Even the Legislature has a judicial character when it undertakes an impeachment process. The Assembly has the power to present the impeachment and the Senate acts as a court in the impeachment trial.

Types of Courts

In the next few pages, we will present a great deal of information on the types of courts in California's system, the jurisdictions, qualifications for judges, and other important facts. To help organize this material, you may find it helpful to study Figure 35 on page 156, which summarizes the key information found in these pages.

Trial and Appellate Courts

In addition to the classifications already discussed, the courts also may be divided into two groups: those which have *original jurisdiction* in cases, and those which primarily hear cases on appeal (*appellate courts*). Superior, Municipal, and Justice Courts are courts of original jurisdiction; in other words, cases are first brought to them. These courts are also known as *trial courts*, because when a case comes to one of them, a trial is conducted, the facts are determined, and a decision is issued. In the appellate (appeal) courts—the California Supreme Court and the Courts of Appeal—cases may be reviewed to determine whether they were fairly and correctly tried in the lower courts.

Municipal and Justice Courts—Inferior Courts

Municipal and Justice courts (also known as *inferior courts*) occupy the bottom level of the court system. The difference between the two is simply that Justice Courts serve rural areas and Municipal Courts serve urban areas. Each county is divided into municipal and justice court districts by its Board of Supervisors. A city cannot be divided into more than one district, but each Municipal and Justice Court may have one or more judges. Municipal Courts are for districts of over 40,000 residents, Justice Courts for districts of under 40,000. The Legislature establishes the number of judges for each district and determines their salaries and qualifications. (In November 1974 California voters approved a change permitting any city in San Diego county to be divided into more than one municipal court or justice court district, providing the legislature approves.)

Election of Judges

Judges for both Municipal and Justice Courts are elected to serve six-year terms by the people of their district in open general elections. Vacancies on Municipal Courts are filled by the Governor; the Board of Supervisors calls a special election or appoints a justice to fill a Justice Court vacancy.

Jurisdiction in civil cases in Municipal Courts ordinarily is limited to cases involving less than $5,000 and in Justice Courts to cases under $1,000. These courts also may hear criminal cases if they involve misdemeanors of county or municipal ordinances or laws. The two inferior courts also conduct preliminary hearings on felony charges, to determine whether an offense has been committed and if sufficient cause exists to believe the accused is guilty. If the judge believes both to be true, then the case is tried in a Superior Court.

Small Claims Court.   Both Municipal and Justice Courts also serve as Small Claims Courts. Small Claims Courts were created in the 1920s, to provide an inexpensive, speedy, and informal way to settle disputes involving minor amounts of money. They began as an effort to aid the poor in resolving claims. The judge investigates the controversy, examines the evidence, and makes the judgment. Lawyers cannot represent the parties involved, so legal fees are eliminated. These courts were designed to help those who cannot afford a lawyer, but recently they have been used by landlords, department stores, insurance companies, and institutional creditors in general. One of the basic reasons this has occurred stems from the continual rise in the amount defined as a small claim. By 1970, the maximum amount within the definition was up to $500 (from its original $50), and recommendations were being made to push it higher, perhaps to as much as $1,000. This increase has encouraged more and more institutional creditors to take advantage of these courts to collect on their customers' unpaid bills. Average individuals seem less and less to make use of the benefits of the courts' informal and inexpensive nature.

Superior Court

The California Constitution requires that one Superior Court be established for each county. The Legislature decides the number of judges to serve

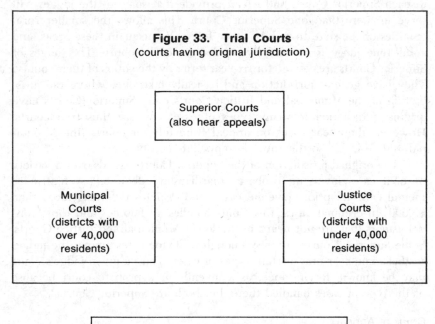

Figure 33.   Trial Courts
(courts having original jurisdiction)

Superior Courts
(also hear appeals)

Municipal
Courts
(districts with
over 40,000
residents)

Justice
Courts
(districts with
under 40,000
residents)

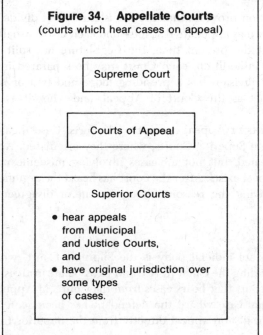

Figure 34.   Appellate Courts
(courts which hear cases on appeal)

Supreme Court

Courts of Appeal

Superior Courts

• hear appeals
  from Municipal
  and Justice Courts,
  and
• have original jurisdiction over
  some types
  of cases.

in each Superior Court, and it can provide that some of the judges will serve in more than one Superior Court. This allows the smaller rural counties of the state to reduce costs; few cases occur in these areas, and a full-time judge is not usually needed for each county. The judges of Superior Courts are elected for six-year terms by the voters of their county. They have general jurisdiction and basically take over where the juris- diction of the Municipal and Justice Courts ends. Superior Courts have original jurisdiction in many types of cases and are thus trial courts. However, they hear cases on appeal from inferior courts (the Munici- pal–Justice level), so they are also appellate courts.

The original jurisdiction of the Superior Court extends over a variety of civil cases involving probate, guardianship, divorce, psychiatric or mental care, adoption, juvenile cases, and disputes involving more than $5,000. In criminal cases, this Court handles all felonies and those mis- demeanors that are not heard in the lower Municipal and Justice Courts. Some Superior Courts are busy enough to divide cases among the judges so that some hear only certain types of cases. Thus, a given judge's court may be known, for instance, as a juvenile or a probate court because of the type of cases handled there, but both are Superior Courts.

Court of Appeal

The Constitution provides that the Legislature shall divide the state into districts—known as appellate districts—and each district shall have a Court of Appeal. At the present time, the Legislature has split the state into five districts. In addition, each Court may be separated into divisions if needed. Each division has a presiding judge and two or more associate judges who act as the Court of Appeal, and who sit as a three-judge court.

The Courts of Appeal are not trial courts. Cases heard there come on appeal from Superior Courts, where they originated. Any felony case may be appealed, but not all cases involving misdemeanors can be, if a basis for appeal exists. After the court has heard the arguments, it renders a decision, giving the reasons for agreement or disagreement with the lower court.

Supreme Court

The highest state judicial body is the Supreme Court, which has seven members including the Chief Justice and six associate justices. It is primarily an appellate court that hears cases from the Courts of Appeal. One excep- tion is that any case where the defendant has been sentenced to death goes automatically on appeal directly from the Superior to the Supreme Court.

The Supreme Court also may order that any case before a Court of Appeal be transferred to it, or to another Court of Appeal. The reason for doing so is that the Supreme Court considers the case to be one of special urgency or public importance. Through such interventions, the Court can involve itself in cases that have significant legal considerations, or where uniformity and consistency in the law need to be maintained.[1]

Appeals

It is important to remember that an appellate court has the power to set aside a decision of a lower court and to order a new trial. This action is taken only after the appellate court has examined the entire case and all the evidence and determined that the lower court's decision was unjust or incomplete. A case can be appealed for any of several reasons—for example, the jury may have been misdirected by the judge, or evidence may have been improperly admitted or rejected.

Qualifications and the State Bar

In order to be selected as a judge of a court of record (any except a Justice Court), a person has to be a member of the State Bar or have served as a judge of a court of record in California. A municipal court judge must have been a member for the five years preceding his selection, and judges of Superior Courts, Courts of Appeal, and the Supreme Court for the ten preceding their selection.

A Justice Court judge need not be either a member of the State Bar or have served as a judge of a court of record. This means judges of this court need not be attorneys; they may be ordinary citizens who act as judges on a part-time basis. At present, they are required to pass an examination in order to qualify for office.

In mid-August 1974, the California Supreme Court acted to restrict the activity of these nonlawyer Justice Court judges. In a decision that certainly will cause court reform bills to be considered in future legislative sessions, the Court said that nonlawyer judges could not preside in criminal cases that might result in a jail sentence without the consent of the defendant. Because this ruling severely restricts the role of these judges, and therefore, the activity of Justice Courts, these courts and the qualifications of the presiding judges undoubtedly will be rethought and reworked.

The State Bar is a public corporation that is part of the judicial branch and is under the supervision of the Supreme Court. Every person who is licensed to practice law in California must be a member. However, when he holds office as a judge of a court of record, a lawyer ceases to be a member of the Bar. The Bar establishes the requirements for

Figure 35. The California Court System

Type of Court	Jurisdiction	Who Selects Judges?	Term of Office?	Who Fills Vacancies?	Qualifications Required?
Supreme Court (one for entire state)	Appeals from Courts of Appeal (and cases involving death penalty, which are appealed automatically and directly from Superior Courts)	Governor nominates; state's voters say yes or no	12 years	Governor	Member of State Bar for 10 years preceeding selection, or judge of a court of record
Courts of Appeal (five districts for entire state)	Appeals from Superior Courts—mostly felonies	Governor nominates; district's voters say yes or no	12 years	Governor	Member of State Bar for 10 years preceding selection, or judge of a court of record
Superior Courts (one for each county; each may be subdivided into Probate Court, Juvenile Court, and so on)	Both *appeals* from Justice and Municipal Courts and *original jurisdiction:* *Civil:* probate, guardianship, divorce, psychiatric care, adoption, juvenile, cases involving over $5,000 *Criminal:* all felonies, and misdemeanors not heard in lower courts	Voters of the county: open nonpartisan election	6 years	Governor	Member of State Bar for 10 years preceding selection, or judge of a court of record
Municipal Courts (may be several in each county—one for each *urban* district of over 40,000 people; the city of San Diego may have two districts)	Original jurisdiction over —civil cases involving less than $5,000, and —criminal cases involving misdemeanor violations of county or municipal laws Hold preliminary hearings (not trials) on felony charges Act as small claims courts	Voters of the district; open nonpartisan election	6 years	Governor	Member of State Bar for 5 years preceding selection, or judge of a court of record
Justice Courts (may be several in each county—one for each *rural* district of under 40,000 people; the city of San Diego may have two districts)	Similar to Municipal Courts, except civil cases limited to those involving less than $1,000 Hold preliminary hearings (not trials) on felony charges Act as small claims courts	Voters of the district; open nonpartisan election	6 years	Board of Supervisors appoints successor or calls special election	Need not be a member of State Bar; must pass examination

an individual to practice law in California, and administers any examination or hearing where potential attorneys attempt to qualify. The Bar then reports to the Supreme Court the names of those who have qualified, and the Court admits them to the Bar. The Bar also reviews any charges of misconduct by attorneys, and attempts to maintain professional standards among lawyers.

Vacancies, Elections, and Terms

Judges' terms of office and the methods for filling vacancies and electing judges for various types of courts are summarized in Figure 35 on page 156, because the information is easier to learn in that form than in descriptive form.

In addition, it is important to recognize the difference between the two types of elections used to select judges for different court levels. One type is a regular, open election (but in this case nonpartisan) like those used for other public offices, in which voters directly select the judge from a number of possible candidates. This system is used for the election of Superior, Municipal, and Justice Court judges.

The second type of election takes the form of a simple question on the ballot: Shall this candidate be elected? Voters answer yes or no, but that is the only choice. No other candidate is presented. If a majority of voters agree to the candidate, he is elected. If not, the Governor must nominate another candidate for the position. This indirect election system is used only for the Supreme Court and Courts of Appeal.

If an incumbent judge on the Supreme Court or a Court of Appeal decides to run for another term, he may file what is known as a declaration of candidacy, and his name will then be placed on the ballot in the yes–no form described above. If he does not choose to run again, the Governor nominates a new name for the position.

Reform Suggestions

This whole election system has been widely criticized, and several suggestions have been made to change it. One proposed reform of the nomination system suggests that appointments be made by the Governor from a list of names drawn up by special commissions. These commissions would carefully screen candidates and supply the Governor with a small list of names from which he could choose the new judge. The idea here is that political pressure would be at least somewhat removed from the proceedings, and selection could be done on the basis of merit alone.

Critics have charged that the competitive local campaigns for judges are an inappropriate method for selection because the campaign is likely to focus not on legal matters, but on personality conflicts and other nonlegal issues. Instead, it is suggested that a screening committee review possible candidates, draw up a list of nominees, and submit it to the Governor. From that list, the Governor would nominate candidates for Superior, Municipal, and Justice Courts. Once nominated, a judge for these courts would be subject to election in the same fashion judges for the Supreme Court and Courts of Appeal are. That is, voters would be asked to say yes or no as to whether the judge should serve. This reform would eliminate open campaigning and help to make certain that only qualified candidates become judges.

Also, it is obvious that any Governor now has a mighty influence over California's court system through his power of appointment to fill vacancies. A governor can reward friends, political supporters, and other politicians with judgeships, and he can appoint only individuals with a particular political outlook and philosophy. Legal knowledge and ability in such cases may be a decidedly secondary consideration. The use of a screening committee to suggest nominees might be a substantial step toward overcoming this rather unhealthy situation.

Commission on Judicial Appointments

One check currently exists to control the quality of judicial appointees. The Governor nominates and appoints judges to fill vacancies on the Supreme Court and Courts of Appeal, but those appointments do not become effective until reviewed and confirmed by the Commission on Judicial Appointments. This commission has three members: the Chief Justice of the Supreme Court, the state's Attorney General, plus the presiding justice of the district affected by the appointment. If the nomination or appointment is to the Supreme Court, the presiding justice who has served the longest on any Court of Appeal joins the Chief Justice and Attorney General as the third member.

Controversy During the Reagan Administration

In January 1973, then-Governor Ronald Reagan appointed to a vacancy on the Supreme Court Judge William A. Clark, Jr., from the Court of Appeal in Los Angeles. Clark, it turned out, had been a member of Reagan's staff in 1967 and 1968. In 1969, Reagan had appointed him to the Superior Court of San Luis Obispo County. About two years later he had appointed him to the Court of Appeal in Los Angeles. After spending about a year and a half on that court, he was appointed to the Supreme Court.

This rapid rise seemed remarkable to some critics who believed the Governor was merely looking out for a friend. Reagan contended Clark had had a brilliant career as a lawyer for 15 years, but critics labeled his career as undistinguished. In fact, it was revealed that because of poor grades, Clark had been forced to leave law school and had never graduated from any of the universities he had attended. He had passed the State Bar examination, but only after taking it a second time. It also was pointed out that several of his decisions as a Superior Court judge and Appeal Court judge had been overruled by higher courts. In the critics' view, Supreme Court justices needed a thorough knowledge of the law in order to make the important decisions expected of the Court, and Clark, they said, did not seem to have that kind of knowledge. Reagan actively defended his appointment, and Clark supporters emerged to stress his willingness to learn and his great dedication. They also believed that his critics were simply snobs who objected because the judge had never graduated from a law school.

Because the nomination proved to be so very controversial, the Chief Justice of the Supreme Court asked the State Bar to examine Clark's qualifications. The Bar review concluded that no reasons existed to disqualify the nomination, although it did state that the majority of people interviewed were highly concerned that Clark had demonstrated no great ability as a judge, and did not seem to be the quality of judge needed to serve on the Supreme Court. In addition, three law school faculties objected to the Clark appointment. At a public hearing held by the Commission, praise as well as criticism of Clark was voiced. The day after the hearing, the Commission voted 2–1 to confirm Clark. The one opposing vote was that of the Chief Justice.[2]

Other Commission Decisions

The controversy surrounding this appointment and the interest in this Commission were unheard of. Not since the 1940s had such an incident occurred. In 1940, the Commission had refused confirmation of the Governor's appointment of a University of California law professor to the Supreme Court. That is the only time since the Commission's creation in 1934 that a Governor's appointment was rejected.

In 1974, a Reagan nominee to fill a vacancy on a Court of Appeal also aroused considerable controversy. The State Bar came out against the appointment, and at a hearing by the Commission on Judicial Appointments, the nominee drew praise as well as considerable criticism, particularly on the grounds that he lacked both judicial experience and actual courtroom trial experience. (Only a handful of his cases ever went to court.) Opponents suggested that such experience was particularly needed by appellate judges. Reagan withdrew the nomination at the appointee's request—the first such withdrawal since 1942.

The Commission on Judicial Qualifications

The Commission on Judicial Qualifications is a nine-member body that was established in 1960. It can recommend that the Supreme Court remove or retire any judge, on the bases shown in Figure 36.

The Supreme Court has several times censured judges, and removed some from office for felony convictions. But in 1973, for the first time the Commission recommended that a Municipal Judge be removed for willful misconduct in office and for conduct prejudicial to the administration

---

Figure 36.   The Commission on Judicial Qualifications

The nine members of the Commission are chosen as follows:

Supreme Court Appoints:
- two judges from Courts of Appeal
- two judges from Superior Courts
- one Municipal Court judge.

Board of Governors of State Bar Appoints:
- two lawyers who have practiced in California for at least ten years.

Governor Appoints:
- two citizens who are neither judges, retired judges, nor members of the Bar. (His appointments must be approved by a majority of the Senate.)

The Commission may recommend to the Supreme Court several kinds of actions:

Suspension from Office
- if a judge pleads guilty or no contest to a felony, or is found guilty of a felony.

Retirement
- if a judge suffers a potentially permanent disability that seriously interferes with the performance of his duties.

Censure or Removal from Office
- for willful misconduct
- for willful and persistent failure to perform his duties
- for habitual drunkenness
- for conduct prejudicial to the administration of justice that brings the judicial office into disrepute.

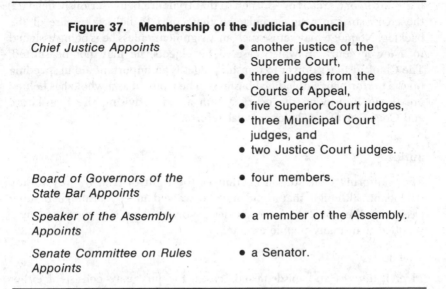

Figure 37.   Membership of the Judicial Council

Chief Justice Appoints

- another justice of the Supreme Court,
- three judges from the Courts of Appeal,
- five Superior Court judges,
- three Municipal Court judges, and
- two Justice Court judges.

Board of Governors of the State Bar Appoints

- four members.

Speaker of the Assembly Appoints

- a member of the Assembly.

Senate Committee on Rules Appoints

- a Senator.

of justice that brings the judicial office into disrepute. This judge was declared unfit not on grounds of dishonesty or corruption but because of his rather crude, base conduct as a judge in and about the courtroom. An appeal to the United States Supreme Court failed to change the decision.

The Judicial Council

Beside these two Commissions—one to oversee appointments and the other to review the fitness of judges to remain in office—California has a Judicial Council, whose duty it is to improve the administration of justice in the state.[3] The Council's 21 members are appointed as shown in Figure 37 with all members except the Chief Justice serving for two-year terms. (The Chief Justice is the Chairman and is a member as long as he is Chief Justice.)

The Council conducts surveys of judicial business, makes yearly recommendations to the Governor and Legislature on ways to improve the judicial process, and adopts rules for court administration, practice, and procedure. To help carry out its duties, the Council appoints an executive officer known as the Administrative Director of the Courts.

The Role of the Chief Justice

As chairman of the Council, the Chief Justice must help to speed up the process of judicial business and to equalize judges' workloads. Thus, if a court in one area is overloaded so that trials are being seriously delayed, the chairman can assign a judge to that court to help take care of the backlog. No judge may refuse such an assignment unless he is being assigned to a lower court, in which case, if he objects, he may not be shifted. The Chief Justice's power to transfer judges is an important aid in speeding up the performance of judicial business. The Council as a whole has helped greatly in improving the court system and in advising the Legislature and Governor of needs for judicial reform.

Juries

The California Constitution guarantees the right of trial by jury to any defendant, although that right may be waived in any criminal or civil case with the consent of the parties involved. This is a more common practice than many people assume.

Trial Juries

In civil actions and misdemeanor cases, the jury may consist of either 12 or any lesser number of people that the parties involved agree upon. Juries in criminal cases must have 12 members. Juries are made up of people whose names have been gathered at random and placed on a list of qualified people. (Qualifications are listed in Figure 38.) From this list individuals are summoned to serve on specific juries.

Figure 38.   Jury Qualifications

To qualify as a juror a person must
- be a United States citizen;
- be 18 years old;
- be a resident of the state and county or city and county for one year before being selected;
- be in possession of his natural faculties, of ordinary intelligence, and not decrepit;
- have sufficient knowledge of English.

Grand Juries

In addition to such trial juries, the California Constitution requires that a *grand jury* be formed and called at least once a year in each county. Counties with populations of over 4 million have 23-member grand juries, those with smaller populations have 19-member juries. The jury is formed by drawing at random from a grand jury box containing the names of qualified persons who have been interviewed in the Superior Court.

A grand jury serves for one year, beginning July 1, and reviews both civil and criminal proceedings. Its task is to hear evidence and witnesses to determine whether a crime has been committed. If this is found to be the case, the jury returns an indictment against the individual believed to have committed the crime. This process takes the place of the preliminary hearings, which do the same thing in inferior courts. The big difference between grand jury hearings and other preliminary hearings is that the grand jury meets secretly and hears only the presentation of evidence by the prosectuion. The person accused is not present, and neither is his attorney. Therefore, no strong defense is presented, and the evidence is not reviewed from the point of view of the accused.

Grand juries also may investigate activities involving county government and make recommendations for improvements. The 1973 Los Angeles County Grand Jury, for example, dealt with nuclear generating plants, Juvenile Hall conditions, the creation of the office of county mayor, and the indictment of the Los Angeles County Marshal. In addition, the county Board of Supervisors asked the jury to study the energy crisis and the activities of oil companies and to examine charges of political influence in awarding county architectural contracts.

Judicial Reform

This chapter already has discussed some recent efforts at judicial reform and suggestions for improvement. This section will explore other suggestions for change and improved functioning of the California court system.[4]

Grand Juries

Grand juries have been criticized because they do not reflect all segments of the community they supposedly represent. A large proportion of grand jurors tend to be from the better educated, older, more affluent members of any given community. Such people may find it difficult to understand the problems of racial minorities or the poor, who may make up a large number of those whom the jury indicts.

The 1974–75 Los Angeles Grand Jury well illustrates the problem. The average age of the jury members was 59, and of the 23 members, 90 percent were either housewives or were retired. Originally, the county's 161 Superior Court judges nominated a list of 212 persons, 77 percent of whom were retired or homemakers. A drawing reduced this list to 40, and from that list the 23 names were chosen. Of the 11 women serving, 9 were housewives; of the 12 men, 9 were retired.

In order to avoid such problems in San Francisco the Superior Court asked for grand jury volunteers. Over 400 people responded, and the final

19-member jury selected had a majority of volunteers. The problem of filling a grand jury stems from the time-consuming nature of its activities. The San Francisco jurors mentioned above faced a year of service, meeting semi-weekly for $10 a meeting. The length of service, the numerous meetings, and the extremely low pay mean that few working-class individuals can afford to serve. To reform this setup so that grand juries represent a cross-section of the community will be a hard task.

Trial Juries

Problems also exist for the trial jury. Many jurors are unfamiliar with court proceedings, and critics have questioned jurors' ability to carry out their duties. Suggestions for reform of the trial jury include the following: (1) require a brief school for jurors to familiarize them with court procedures; (2) limit jurors' decision making to the determination of facts, leaving it to the judge to decide the law; and (3) hire experts to advise the jury in its discussions.

Another proposal calls for reducing the size of the trial jury for criminal cases, for instance, from 12 to 6, to promote efficiency. Another suggests allowing split votes rather than requiring unanimous verdicts to decide criminal cases. Both of these ideas would, of course, seriously alter the present working of the trial jury, but they would allow speedier deliberations and help prevent criminals and their attorneys from abusing the trial jury setup by selecting one or two individuals for a jury who they believe would prevent a unanimous verdict.

At the heart of many such proposals is the idea that jury trials allow criminals to get off too lightly. Perhaps judges could handle cases more effectively, but in felony cases, 74 percent of jury decisions are convictions while judges convict only 59 percent.[5]

Court Backlogs

One serious problem has been the large backlog of cases that develops in the courts. A major reform attempted in the Legislature (which failed) was aimed at combining the Justice, Municipal, and Superior Courts into one Superior Court. The purpose was to improve the efficiency of this level of the judicial system by ending any conflicts of purpose and action among the three courts.

Some individuals stress the need for greater court efficiency but ignore the fact that the justice system provides a series of checks and balances. It is necessarily set up to provide due process and a fair trial. Should society decrease the rights of the accused in the name of efficiency? This is a vital question to answer; many proposed changes in the jury concept and other basic ideas would radically change the workings of the present system.

In addition, the courts' backlog may not be as serious as critics have charged. Recent reviews show that it has lessened considerably, and the courts themselves are moving to adopt procedures to reduce that backlog. Among these are better examinations at preliminary hearings, and the use of Municipal Court Judges at the Superior court level to handle case overloads. These practices are already in use and they are working. Figure 39 shows some of the important myths and facts about court efficiency.

Figure 39.   Conditions in California's Courts

Myth	*Fact*
• The courts are becoming more and more crowded.	• California courts are becoming less crowded.
• Judges are increasingly overburdened. New judgeships cannot solve this.	• Judges' workloads have decreased.
• New cases come in faster than the courts can dispose of old ones.	• New filings have decreased, but the Superior Courts in 1971–72 handled a record number of cases, 4252 more than in the previous year.
• The trial court system is an enormous financial drain on the taxpayer.	• California's courts make money. In one recent year they made $31 million beyond their expenses.
• The courts are coddling criminals.	• Most criminal defendants are convicted. The conviction rate for robbery is 86.9 percent and for burglary is 91.2 percent.
• More and more criminal cases are crowding the courts.	• A marked drop in the volume of criminal cases has occurred.
• Jury trials in criminal cases place a great burden on the courts.	• Very few criminal cases are decided by juries, and the number of criminal jury

trials has decreased. (Only 7 percent of the felony cases in Superior Courts in 1971–72 were handled by juries.)

• Criminal defendants want jury trials because their chances of getting off are better.

• 74 percent of all jury verdicts in felony cases are convictions. For cases tried by judges, 59 percent of the verdicts are convictions.

• Jury trials cost the taxpayer a fortune.

• Even considering only expenses and ignoring court revenues, the annual cost for all felony jury trials runs to less than 15 cents per state inhabitant.

From Coleman A. Blease and Harriet Katz Berman, "Should the Courts Run on Time?" published by the American Civil Liberties Union.

Sources: Judicial Council of California, *Annual Report*, January 1972 and January 1973. Bureau of Criminal Statistics, State of California Department of Justice, *Felony Defendants Disposed of in California Courts*, July 1972.

Justice Courts

In the late 1960s and early 1970s critics strongly attacked Justice Court operations, particularly the fact that this court's judges did not have to be lawyers. Bills introduced in the Legislature to restrict the activity of nonlawyer judges and to unify all trial courts, thus virtually eliminating Justice Courts, failed to pass. However, a mid-August 1974 California Supreme Court decision reopened the reform effort. The Court, as noted earlier in this chapter, severely limited the role of nonlawyer Justice Court judges. Very simply, the California Supreme Court agreed with the critics. Criminal law in particular has grown increasingly complex, and nonlawyer judges are hard pressed to deal effectively with the intricacies of modern criminal trial proceedings. The Court decision left these judges with jurisdiction over civil matters and only those criminal cases where the defendant agreed to the nonlawyer judge presiding. Because just under 130 nonlawyers hold these judgeships, and because in 12 rural northern California counties these courts are directed only by nonlawyers and have no Municipal Courts to pick up the caseload, new court reform legislation is a certainty for the mid-1970s. In the meantime special legislation has provided for temporary circuit judgeships to take the cases nonlawyer judges will not be able to handle.[6]

A 1973 case in a Justice Court in Calaveras County perhaps shows the problems of such a court. The part-time judge of the San Andreas court became involved in a conflict with the editor and publisher of the local newspaper. After the editor publicly criticized the judge's actions in a case relating to a dog trespassing in the judge's garden, the judge attempted to haul the editor into court over his editorial. The editor then appealed to a Superior Court, which ruled that the Justice Court judge could not charge the editor for his editorial. To court reformers, this case seemed to illustrate what can happen when nonlawyer judges are in charge of courts. Their inexperience in legal matters may make the court process appear laughable.[7]

Court Issues

Several recent court decisions have stimulated and increased interest in the court system and its importance. In particular, the California Supreme Court, over a period of many years, has established the reputation of being willing to take on controversial matters and issue equally controversial opinions. It has made important decisions affecting California abortion laws, school financing, the death penalty, reapportionment, and the environment. Almost all of this Court's decisions have either been unanimous or 6–1 votes. Only a very few are close or 4–3 decisions. That is an important point because it means that the Court is rarely divided in its decisions and that it attempts to reach a consensus in order to present a unified, solid view. Another interesting feature of the Court is its willingness to review its earlier decisions and alter them if necessary. This has had the effect of keeping the Court active, and it demonstrates the Court's great interest in preventing a miscarriage of justice.[8]

The Death Penalty

The California Supreme Court's handling of the death penalty is a clear example of the Court's willingness to reconsider previous decisions. The Court upheld the constitutionality of the death penalty in 1968, but later decided to review its position. In February 1972, it ruled that the death penalty constituted cruel or unusual punishment and violated the California Constitution. The 1968 ruling was a 4–3 decision; the 1972 vote was 6–1. Some of the justices had changed their positions. One of those who changed his opinion was the Justice who had written the 1968 ruling upholding the death penalty.

The reaction to the death penalty decision was instant. The Governor and the Attorney General strongly criticized the Court. Almost immediately, a constitutional amendment re-establishing the death penalty was introduced into the Legislature, where it failed to pass. An initiative constitutional amendment (Proposition 17) was approved by the voters in the November 1972 general election, but the issue remained unresolved. Previously, in June 1972, the United States Supreme Court had ruled the death penalty was not unconstitutional in terms of the federal Constitution, but had struck down all California death penalty provisions except for those that provided for a mandatory death sentence. Thus, the 1973 Legislature, under heavy pressure, passed new legislation making the death penalty mandatory for 11 kinds of killings.

School Financing

Another subject the Court took on was that of school financing. In August 1968, a suit had been filed by John Serrano, Jr., and some other parents on behalf of their children. Their suit (known as *Serrano* v. *Priest*)[9] charged that because of different tax rates among school districts and the resulting wide variations of spending on each child, educational opportunity depended strictly upon where a student lived. Therefore, they said, their children were denied their right to equal protection under the law. As previously discussed in Chapter Two, the original case was thrown out of Superior Court. An appeal to the Supreme Court held that the present system of educational financing was unconstitutional. The Superior Court was directed to decide whether large differences in spending did exist, and whether or not the quality of education also varied as a result.

The *Serrano* decision forced the Legislature to try to find a more equal way to support California schools, and in 1972 it passed a bill designed to do that. But in May 1974, when the Superior Court ended its review of educational financing, it ruled that both the original financing method and the 1972 reform were unconstitutional, and that better financing measures were needed. The real result of the *Serrano* decision was to force the state government to take on a larger role in financing public schools in order to avoid the effects of inequality in local tax rates and the resultant funds available to spend on pupils.

Reapportionment

The Supreme Court also has involved itself in the problem of the reapportionment of legislative and congressional districts. As stated earlier, the Legislature attempted to reapportion itself in 1971, but the Governor vetoed the bill, stating that it was written to preserve Democratic control of the Legislature and did nothing for Republicans. The immediate problem was that 1972 elections could not be held until at least a tentative solution was reached.

The Supreme Court ruled that because five new congressional seats were due California as a result of population growth, the reapportionment of the congressional districts (which added the five new seats) would have to be used for the 1972 election. At the same time, candidates for Senate and Assembly seats were to run in the old districts. The Court then waited for the Legislature to pass a new bill in 1972, but retained jurisdiction in the case to draft reapportionment plans for the 1974–80 elections if the Legislature should fail to resolve the matter.[10]

In 1972, no new reapportionment plan passed the Legislature. When the 1973 Legislature meetings began, an urgent, all-out drive was started to pass a reapportionment bill, because the Court was to draw up its own plan if no legislative solution were reached. In May 1973, the Court declared it would move to draft its own reapportionment plan but would consider any legislative bill. In June, the Legislature sent Governor Reagan a reapportionment bill, which he promptly vetoed, strongly objecting on the basis that the proposed Assembly districts had been gerrymandered.

As a result, the Court had to reapportion the districts. It previously had appointed three special masters to conduct hearings on reapportionment, draw up and present a plan to the Court by August 31, 1973. The three masters—two retired Superior Court judges and a retired judge from the Court of Appeal—completed the plan.

The Supreme Court conducted hearings on the proposed remapping of legislative boundaries, and in late November 1973 it was ordered into effect. Several unique elements characterized the plan. It was drawn up strictly on a population basis, ignoring the position of incumbents, who then faced a battle to retain their seats. Two side effects emerged. One was to create a Senate district in Los Angeles that would no doubt elect a black person—the second for the Senate. And a Senate district was created in the Mexican-American area of East Los Angeles, making the election of a Mexican-American from this area a distinct possibility.[11]

This was the first court-created redistricting plan in California history. It placed the Supreme Court in the position of drawing district boundaries, a very political act. Once more, the Court had refused to back away from a very controversial issue—this time, that of legislative reapportionment.

Environmental Issues

The California Supreme Court has also become involved in several environmental issues. One important recent ruling already discussed in Chapter Two was the 1972 *Friends of Mammoth* case. The law in dispute was the California Environmental Quality Act (EQA), which requires environmental impact statements before any major construction projects are approved.

Friends of Mammoth.   The dispute was over whether private as well as public projects were included in the scope of the EQA. Did a government agency have to give permission to proceed with a private project that was going to have a direct influence on the environment? The Supreme Court had to determine how broadly the word "project" was to be used. It decided that the term did include both public and private projects, and as a result, the Legislature passed additional legislation clarifying the meaning of the law and including the Court's decision.[12]

Environmentalist Foes Appear.   The controversy over the EQA illustrates a bigger problem in which the Supreme Court and other courts have become involved. Environmentalist groups have decided that if they do not win by pressuring the executive and legislative branches, they will bring lawsuits to press their views. Several groups were most concerned over the environmentalist position. Both labor and management groups, especially those in the building and construction industry, feared that environmentalists' actions would restrict state growth and slow or halt the work of business, especially the construction industry.

In 1973, the Pacific Legal Foundation was formed by a group of businessmen and lawyers. The idea had first been suggested to the California Chamber of Commerce, which had decided that although the idea was a good one, the Chamber could not handle it. Thus the private foundation was formed. One of its basic purposes is to fight the work of environmentalists, on the grounds that their interests are quite special and narrow. The Foundation is to represent a more balanced view in defense of both government agencies and industrial, business, and agricultural interests in environmental lawsuits.[13]

As environmentalist pressures increase and as, for example, the problems of air pollution and water pollution worsen, the legal side of the problems also will increase. And in the thick of those legal problems will be environmentalist lawyers, lawyers representing business and industry (like the Pacific Legal Foundation), and the courts themselves—including the Supreme Court.

Issues Reveal Future Trends

What is the importance of examining issues such as these? This discussion shows that the major issues of the 1970s will include heated battles in the California court system as well as in the legislative and executive branches. The appearance of organizations such as the Pacific Legal Foundation, and the willingness of groups such as environmentalists to appear in court to argue for their positions will only aid in drawing the courts more and more into the considerations of these issues. Thus, the court system is as important a factor in resolving these issues as are the other two branches. Judicial procedures and operations, therefore, need to be understood as well as those of the legislative and executive branches. All three are involved in meeting the problems of California's world.

Review Questions

How many levels of courts exist in California?

What is a court of record?

What governmental bodies have court-like functions?

What is the difference between an appellate court and a trial court? List the appellate and trial courts in the California system.

What is original jurisdiction?

What are the functions of Municipal and Justice Courts? How do the two courts differ?

What is the difference between a misdemeanor and a felony?

Give some examples of the original jurisdiction of the Superior Court. Does it have an appellate function?

What is the highest court in the state? How many judges serve on this court? What sorts of cases does it handle?

What qualifications must one have to be a judge?

What is the California State Bar?

Who fills the vacancies on courts of record?

What is the difference between the election process for the Supreme Court and Courts of Appeal, and for the Superior and Municipal Courts?

What does the Commission on Judicial Appointments do?

What does the Commission on Judicial Qualifications do?

What is the Judicial Council? Why is it important?

What is the difference between a trial jury and a grand jury?

List some recent controversial issues in which the Supreme Court has become involved.

Notes

1. The *California Journal* interview with the Chief Justice, 2 (December, 1971): 334–336, touches on many of the points referred to in this chapter. For other information on the Supreme Court, see also *California Journal* 5 (April, 1974): 116–119; *Los Angeles Times*, October 27, 1974.

2. Dennis Campbell, "How Is Reagan's Alter-Ego Making It on the Wright Court?" *California Journal* 5 (April, 1974): 117–119.

3. "Judicial Council Seeks to Reduce Court Congestion, Develop Uniform System of Judicial Administration," *California Journal* 2 (December, 1971): 337–338, 347.

4. Bethami Auerbach, "Major Court Reorganization Proposal Heads Toward Senate Showdown," *California Journal* 2 (July–August, 1971): 196–198.

5. Coleman A. Blease and Harriet Katz Berman, "Should the Courts Run on Time?" American Civil Liberties Union; see also *California Journal* 4 (September, 1973): 309–311, for a broader review of the problems mentioned here.

6. *Sacramento Bee*, August 15 and 16, 1974.

7. *Sacramento Bee*, February 2, 4, and 15, 1973.

8. The *Los Angeles Times*, June 18, 1973, carried an article on the Court and its procedures which was helpful in preparing this section; Winifred L. Hepperle, "*People* v. *Sharp:* A Look Behind the Court's Blue Velvet Curtain," *California Journal* 3 (August, 1972): 221–223; Ronald Blubough, "A Philosophical Struggle within the Supreme Court," *California Journal* 5 (November, 1974): 382–384. See also *Los Angeles Times*, January 2, 1974, and notes 1 and 2 above.

9. John Serrano, Jr., initiated action on behalf of his son John Anthony Serrano, who was a Baldwin Park elementary school pupil. The defendants included State Treasurer Ivy Baker Priest, State Controller Houston Flournoy, State Superintendent of Public Instruction Wilson Riles, County Tax Collector and Treasurer Harold Ostly, and County Superintendent of Schools Richard Clowes. Denis P. Doyle, "Court Decision Shakes School Tax Structure," *California Journal* 2 (September, 1971): 237, 252, and "*Serrano* v. *Priest,*" 238–239 in the same issue summarize the basic points of this lawsuit. See also the references in Chapter Two, note 14.

10. The original decision is discussed and summarized in the *California Journal* 3 (January, 1972): 7–11.

11. Ed Salzman, "Masters' Redistricting Outlook," *California Journal* 4 (October, 1973): 333–338; "Final Reapportionment Plan—Or Is It?" *California Journal* 5 (January, 1974): 16–21; Ed Salzman, "Double

Trouble for Republicans—Redistricting and Watergate," *California Journal* 5 (June, 1974): 195–196.

12. See "Court's Ruling on Environmental Impact Reports Puts Pressure on Legislature," *California Journal* 3 (November, 1972): 324–326; *Christian Science Monitor,* April 18, 1973.

13. *Sacramento Bee,* March 4, 1973, April 1, 1973, May 17, 1973, November 5, 1973; *Los Angeles Times,* March 8, 1973. The *Bee* reported a broad thrust by this Foundation to defend government interests against both antipoverty lawyers and ecologists. John Berthelsen, "How Business and Labor Are Challenging the Ecologists," *California Journal* 5 (February, 1974): 59–61.

CHAPTER SEVEN

LOCAL GOVERNMENT

Overview

This chapter has two broad divisions. The first describes the various levels of local government—the types of city and county governments, and what kinds of services they provide. The second part discusses several specific topics—nonpartisanship, lobbying and special interests, local finances, environmental issues, minority group problems, and reform work. From this chapter, you should gain an understanding of the structure of local government and an awareness of what the serious challenges are that face it.

Local governments in California are provided for by the state. In a sense they are an extension of state government, in that the state sets the range of their activities and determines what they may or may not do. The focus of local government, therefore, is narrow.

Local government in California encompasses a variety of government institutions, including cities, counties, and special districts. A special district is one that has only one function—for instance to support and administer schools, libraries, sewage projects, fire protection, police protection, cemeteries, flood control, or street lighting. Special districts may overlap one another. You probably live within the boundaries of several of them. However, for the average citizen, the most familiar and visible local governments are those of the city and county.

County Government

California is divided into 58 counties (see Figure 40) and each Californian lives in a county. County is mandatory, not voluntary; it is required by the state. Before California became so urban, county governments were quite important in enforcing state law within their boundaries and in providing ordinances to meet local conditions. Today, cities tend to have

Figure 40. Counties of California

a more immediate and obvious impact on residents, although county governments still perform many important tasks.

Several of California's counties cover a large area and are bigger than some states. For example, Kern County, only the third largest county in the state, is slightly larger than the state of Massachusetts. California's largest county is San Bernardino, stretching over 20,000 square miles; the smallest is San Francisco, covering just over 40 square miles. The population of the counties also varies considerably. Los Angeles is the largest with approximately 7 million people; the smallest is Alpine, with only about 600. Because of the great differences in size and population, county government varies considerably. The job of governing Los Angeles County—and others of similar size and population—is far more difficult than the administration of a much smaller county, and requires a huge budget and many employees.

County Functions

County government provides general police and fire protection services, supports health services, takes care of recreational needs, operates correctional institutions, and serves as the agent for public welfare by spending money sent to it for that purpose by both state and federal governments. Most recently, county governments also have been faced with rising environmental problems, including the need to preserve open space, handle air and water pollution problems, and deal with sewage and solid waste disposal problems.[1]

Types of County Government

Three kinds of county government are permitted by the California Constitution and all three exist in the state. One is the general law county, the second is the charter county, and the third is a combined city–county charter government.

General Law Counties.   Most (47) of California's counties are general law counties. These, sometimes called statutory counties, have been established in accord with general or statewide laws (statutes) passed by the Legislature. Their operation and function and the officers who are elected or appointed to serve in them are provided for in general laws enacted by the Legislature for all state areas. Initiative and referendum procedures may be used according to Legislature limitations, and each elected official is subject to the recall process.

Charter Counties.   Charter counties are not governed precisely by general laws but according to their charters, which have been established and approved by county voters. Few charter counties exist, but those few include some of the state's most populated areas. In fact, over 13 million of California's nearly 20 million residents live in charter counties. A county charter sets forth the functions and operations of the county. A county may revise and change its charter according to established procedures. While general law counties operate according to legislative acts and therefore by the will of the Legislature, charter counties have a greater degree of self-government and can be more independent. For example, charter counties determine which officers they will have and how they will be selected (elected or appointed). In addition, charter counties decide on the number of special boards and commissions they wish to have and determine how broad the powers of these bodies will be. Basically, a charter permits a county to tailor a government more suited to its local needs than the structure provided for under general law.

Figure 41.   Charter Counties

County	Date Charter Adopted	Population 1970*
Los Angeles	1912	7,040,679
San Bernardino	1912	682,233
Butte	1916	101,969
Tehama	1916	29,517
Alameda	1926	1,073,184
San Francisco	1931	715,674
Fresno	1933	413,329
Sacramento	1933	634,190
San Diego	1933	1,357,854
San Mateo	1933	556,601
Santa Clara	1950	1,066,932
	TOTAL	13,672,162

*Source: *California Statistical Abstract, 1972.*

City–County Governments.   The third and final type of California county structure is the combined city–county, in which city and county governments are merged into a single operation, under a single charter. Such a county has the rights of a charter county and charter city. San Francisco has been the state's only city–county government, but other areas, notably Sacramento, have considered combining city and county operations.

County Officials

The officials of any California county government are basically the same. The major difference is whether a given official is elected or appointed.

Board of Supervisors.   The basic governing body for every county—the Board of Supervisors—*must* be elected. At present, all Boards of Supervisors consist of five members, except for San Francisco's, which has eleven members for its city–county operation. However, any charter county *may* elect more than five supervisors.

Figure 42.   Specific County Needs a Board of Supervisors Can Consider

- Street maintenance
- Sewage disposal
- Fire protection
- Protection of livestock
- Beach, small boat harbor, skiing, and golf course developments
- Rapid transit
- Parks

- Dumps
- Water systems
- Flood control
- County fair
- Airports
- Libraries
- Police work
- Air pollution

Supervisors are elected for staggered four-year terms. That is, every two years elections occur for either two or three members. In general law counties, Supervisors are elected by districts. In order to be elected, they must have lived in their districts for one year and must live there during their term of office. Supervisorial districts must all be about equal in population size. Charter counties may elect Supervisors at large, or they can elect them at large but require each to live in a specific district.

In general law counties, when a vacancy occurs during a term of office, the Governor appoints a new supervisor, who must then run in the *next* general election. In contrast, some charter counties provide that their Boards will fill any vacancies themselves. (This latter procedure is the same as that used in filling vacancies on city councils and boards of special districts.)

What does a Board of Supervisors do? Basically, it is the chief legislative and administrative body for the county. It determines policies to be carried out by county officials, and appoints many of those officials. In addition, it passes ordinances (local county laws) that apply to county areas that are not within the boundary of any city. These ordinances cannot conflict with state laws or deal with topics already well covered by state laws. This latter point is known as preemption. Because of this principle, the Board's lawmaking powers are rather limited.

The Board of Supervisors also approves county expenses, determines the county tax rate, and equalizes tax assessment. In addition, it sells bonds to raise the money needed for county building facilities. Lastly, it supervises county elections, reviews the voting, and formally announces the results.[2]

Chief Administrative Officer.   Besides the Supervisors, a series of other county officers exists. Voters elect far more of these in general law counties than in charter counties, which rely more on electing a few major officials and having the rest appointed. These appointments may be made by the Board of Supervisors or by an officer known as the county manager, county executive, or chief administrative officer.

Only in charter counties can the county manager or county executive office be created. In most cases, this office (however named) is stronger when defined by a county charter than when established by a Board ordinance. In both types of counties, this officer is appointed by the Supervisors to oversee and direct county operations for the Board. He directs the implementation of Board policies and decisions. In some cases, he may make appointments on his own or recommend them to the Board, which makes the final decision. He also serves as a communication link between various departments and the Board. He directs studies for the Board to aid in determining policy and making decisions. In addition, he prepares the budget. In general, he provides the Board with whatever information is necessary for it to carry out its work. In counties that have this chief administrator, he has become an important official.

Other County Officers.   While the county manager or executive is appointed, other officers commonly are elected. These officials include the District Attorney, Sheriff, Assessor, Auditor, Treasurer, and Clerk. They are elected for four-year terms at each gubernatorial election.

The *District Attorney's* prime task is to prosecute violations of the law that occur within the county. He institutes court action to bring about the arrest of persons charged with or suspected of committing public offenses. He also works closely with the grand jury to gain criminal indictments. He also can advise and aid the jury in its investigation of county administration.

In addition, the District Attorney provides legal assistance to various county and district officers, and serves as legal advisor to the Board of Supervisors. In any suit brought against the county, he must defend county interests. All of California's District Attorneys are elected.

Each county elects a *Sheriff,* who oversees general law enforcement activities in county areas: preserving the peace, preventing crime, arresting those who are suspected of committing crimes, preventing disturbances and outbreaks like riots, aiding the Superior Court in its work, taking charge of defendants, and running the county jail.

Each county also elects an *Assessor*, who determines the value of property within the county for tax purposes. He also reports to the State Board of Equalization on assessment practices and regularly provides needed statistical information about the county to this Board for its work.

The *Auditor* acts for the county in much the same way as the state Controller. If a county Controller's office exists, the Auditor holds that position too, as Auditor–Controller. He examines accounts, reviews the Treasurer's books, and issues warrants (checks) that are to be paid from the county treasury.

The county *Treasurer's* functions are quite similar to those of the state treasurer. He receives and keeps county money and pays it out as the law requires when proper warrants are presented. If the county has a *Tax Collector*, he receives the taxes owed the county, and serves as the county *License Collector*, if that office exists.

State law provides that the Board of Supervisors may, with voter approval, create and appoint a *Director of Finance*, who brings together the duties of and replaces the Auditor, Controller, Tax Collector, and Treasurer.

The county *Clerk* may have several important duties, depending on the county. In some counties, he is the clerk for the Board of Supervisors, and he also may serve as clerk to the Superior Court and keep its records. The Clerk also may act as the county registrar of voters and chief election officer. In addition, the Clerk's office collects fees for filing papers, such as for probate proceedings, adoptions, marriage licenses, and articles of incorporation.

Other county government offices include the following:

- The *County Counsel* (when this officer exists) handles all duties of the District Attorney except those of public prosecutor. He is in charge of all civil (noncriminal) legal actions. He advises the Board of Supervisors on legal matters, and represents and advises officers of districts within the county.
- The *Public Defender* represents individuals charged with crimes who cannot afford their own lawyer.
- The *Recorder* records vital statistics (births, deaths, and marriages), mining claims, mortgages, deeds, surveys, charts, and other important papers.
- The *Coroner* investigates all violent, sudden, or unusual deaths, and may conduct a hearing called an inquest. The Coroner may be replaced by an appointed *Medical Examiner*, who is a licensed physician and surgeon and a specialist in pathology.

The list of officials continues and is long, particularly for large or very populous counties. Generally, charter counties elect few officers, relying more on appointed officials to serve. In general law counties, voters face long ballots every four years to elect a rather large group of county officers.

Divided Authority and Responsibility

One of the many problems facing county government is that executive

---

Figure 43. County Officers

Officers required in all counties:

- Members of Board of Supervisors (always elected)
- District Attorney
- Sheriff
- County Clerk
- Assessor
- Public Administrator
- Coroner (may be replaced by appointed Medical Examiner)
- Recorder ⎫
- Tax Collector ⎬ (may be replaced by appointed Director of Finance)
- Auditor ⎪
- Treasurer ⎭

Additional appointive officers:

- Administrative Officer (County Manager, and so on)
- County Health Officer
- County Veterinarian
- Medical Examiner (when established, replaces Coroner)
- County Librarian
- Fish and Game Warden
- License Collector
- Controller
- Director of Finance (when established, replaces Auditor, Tax Collector, Treasurer, and Controller)
- Road Commissioner ⎫
- Surveyor ⎬ (may be replaced by Public Works Director)
- Public Defender
- County Council

Required officers are all elected in General Law counties.

Charter counties may decide to appoint rather than elect some required officers, but Board of Supervisors members are always elected.

General law counties may consolidate offices according to state law—for example, Sheriff may also serve as Tax Collector, Coroner, and/or Public Administrator. District Attorney may serve as Public Administrator and/or Coroner.

Charter counties may consolidate offices in any way they wish.

authority and administrative responsibility are quite divided. Because responsibilities are assigned to a series of elected and appointed officers, it is difficult to pinpoint authority and to maintain centralized goals and a common direction. The Board of Supervisors may hire an administrative officer and other officials to carry out specific Board policies. But elected officials who are not directly responsible to the Board may hinder the establishment of a well-organized and effective administration. They may not choose to follow Board wishes, and the Board cannot force a department run by such elected officials to conform to its will. In this kind of situation, a Board cannot really be held responsible for the total operation of county government, for it lacks the authority in many instances to carry out its tasks.

This situation prevails even though from time to time an office falls vacant during a term, and the Board may have the power to appoint a new official, who will then run at the following election. If he is elected (as happens in most every case), the Board may have elected officials it originally appointed. Nevertheless, that elected official is no longer dependent on the Board—he functions independently of it. It may be argued that when excellent elected officials serve with a less than satisfactory Board, county government better maintains its efficiency and capacity to handle problems, but the greater problem remains: that is, a Board supposedly in charge of county affairs and responsible for leadership lacks the total ability to direct county operations and carry on its work.

City Government

Types of City Government

The other level of local government most noticeable to the average Californian is that of the city. City governments, too, take several different forms: *general law, charter,* and of course the combined *city–county* charter variation already discussed. Most of California's cities are of the general law type—those formed and operated in accord with the laws enacted by the state legislature. In the past, charter cities generally had a greater measure of self-rule than did general law cities. They were better able than general law cities to adapt government to local needs and wishes because they did not have to wait for action by the Legislature. In recent years, however, legislative action has made general law cities provisions less rigid, and now each type has about an equal degree of flexibility. For example, initiative and referendum procedures are equally available to both types of governments.

Like the county, city government is an extension of the state, but in a different way. The state establishes counties and sets up county governments on a mandatory basis, but cities are not required. They come into being only if citizens in an area want to incorporate. Once formed, the city can write a charter and present it for voter approval. If approved by local voters, the charter becomes effective. While a general law city must follow the structure set out in legislative acts, the outline of a charter city's government is drawn up in its charter. Thus, each charter city is different and tends to have its own special structure.

Forms of City Government

Two kinds of city government have been commonly used in California cities, whether charter or general law. One is the *mayor–council* form and the other the *council–manager* form. Cities with a mayor–council structure can be further divided into two groups: strong mayor and weak mayor. This is a matter not so much of the personalities or abilities of the mayors involved, but of the powers given to the office. Strong mayors are elected independently of the city council, and may have substantial appointive or even veto powers. Weak mayors, on the other hand, are usually selected by the council (and may even be council members), and their duties are largely ceremonial.

Mayor–Council.   The governments of California's two largest cities, San Francisco and Los Angeles, happen to be examples of the strong-mayor form of mayor–council government, although the weak-mayor form is far more common in the state. The political importance and desirability of the office are demonstrated in both cities by the large number of candidates who run in each mayoral election. Both cities' mayors have the power to veto council measures and have broad appointment responsibilities, though San Francisco's mayor has greater power in the latter respect.

Even where the city charter gives a mayor a relatively large amount of power, the strength of the office will of course be somewhat determined by the person who holds the office. As discussed in Chapter Two, immediately following his election in 1973, Los Angeles Mayor Tom Bradley showed himself to be an active, determined mayor, becoming vocal and influential in the fight to establish a rapid transit system for the city. In late 1973, he exerted strong leadership to develop a strict emergency plan to deal with the energy crisis. He also used his appointment powers to change substantially the nature of various semi-independent commissions in the city, which are quite important in Los Angeles because they set policy and guide the work of departments such as the airport, fire department, harbor, and police. He used his budget-making responsibility to change the manner in which the budget was drawn up and presented to the council for review. In short, within a year, Bradley had demonstrated that the office of Los Angeles mayor could have considerable power, refuting the complaints of his predecessor, Sam Yorty, that the office was ineffectual because of the city council's ability to override the mayor. Bradley's actions were usually sustained by the Council, whereas Yorty had carried on a running battle with a majority of council members, and his actions *were* often overruled.[3]

The Council–Manager Form.   The most common form of California city government is the council–manager form in which an elected council sets policies and employs a city administrator or manager to implement them. The administrator/manager coordinates the various city offices and their work to make sure council policies are followed. In some cities, he has the power to make appointments to various city positions; in others he recommends appointments to the council, which makes the final appointment decision. Whether the mayor is elected directly by voters or selected by the council from its membership is somewhat unimportant because in either case city administration is actually under the direction of the manager. Some cities have a chief administrative officer who has an even weaker position. He coordinates city work but has little real authority; the council appoints department heads and in general runs the city.

City Officials

Most of California's cities are general law cities with rather simple organization. The major officials are councilmen, a City Clerk, City Treasurer, Chief of Police, Fire Chief, City Attorney, and others. Ordinarily, only the Council, the Clerk, and Treasurer are elected—usually for four-year terms—and the voters can decide to narrow that number even further, electing only the Council and permitting it to select all city officers.

The *city council* may be made up of 5, 7, or 9 members in general law cities, and any number in charter cities (Los Angeles has 15). The council must hold regular meetings, at least once a month. Its appointment responsibilities vary; some or all may be given to a city manager or elected mayor, with or without the right of council approval. The council establishes city policies and passes local ordinances. Such ordinances cannot deal with subjects preempted by the state, or conflict with state laws. (A violation of any local ordinance is a misdemeanor. No local ordinance may carry a fine of over $500 or imprisonment of over 6 months.)

The city *Clerk* maintains the council's records, including those of all ordinances passed. The Clerk is also the accounting officer of the city, and must keep up-to-date records on the city's financial condition. The city *Treasurer* receives and pays out city money, and collects city license fees. The *Chief of Police* has duties similar to those of the county Sheriff, and runs the city jail. If there is a *City Attorney*, he advises officials on all legal matters relating to city business, frames all ordinances, performs any legal services required by the council, and prosecutes misdemeanors committed in the city.

City Functions

Cities usually appear when residents want more services than county government is supplying. They tend to provide the services needed by more urban settings: more police and fire protection, parks, libraries, street maintenance, street lighting, storm drains, garbage and sewage disposal, and rapid transit.

Some California cities contract for many services they need to supply their residents. The idea was developed by the southern California city of Lakewood, which arranged for the County of Los Angeles to provide many needed services (some 41 in total). This contract idea (or Lakewood Plan) appealed to many cities because under such a scheme a city could be established to create all the benefits of local self-rule, while at the same time city taxes could be held to a relatively low level. However, as local governments have begun to charge more for contracted services, interest in such plans has lessened.

A few California cities were formed not to gain the benefits of either local control or more services, but for financial purposes. The City of Industry in Los Angeles County is the most obvious example. Basically, it was created to prevent the area's being added to any surrounding city. In this way, the businesses there avoided paying higher city taxes. This is only one example of the narrow reasons for which cities are sometimes formed.[4]

Special Districts

In addition to California's 58 counties and approximately 400 cities, there exist some 5,000 special districts, organized to handle and usually to carry out a single function. Although school districts are the most visible, an average county resident may live in 15 or more special districts and pay taxes to each one—even though in one combined tax bill. But most Californians do not know what special districts they live in. The boards that govern these districts meet and carry on business as they choose, with little or no public interest in their work. Even elections to these boards often go unnoticed by voters. Yet these districts are important. For one thing, they have the power to set rates for taxes, which the Board of Supervisors must then assess and collect. They set policies that may significantly affect the life style, health, and education of residents—how many libraries the community will have, whether mosquito breeding will be controlled and by what means, whether drain systems will be built to prevent potentially disastrous floods, and a host of other matters. In addition, some districts' boards threatened with being absorbed into larger districts have actively campaigned to avoid being taken over, even when such a merger would benefit the residents whom they represent and perhaps save substantial amounts of money. Thus, it would often greatly benefit taxpayers to increase their awareness of the policies and activities of special districts.

Regional Government

Local government as it now exists tends to look at problems and issues in a piecemeal fashion. It reacts readily to special interests and influences, often ignoring an area's broader needs. To help solve such problems and reduce the number of districts and county and city governments in certain areas, critics have suggested the establishment of *regional* governments. Such structures would consolidate and coordinate many of the duties and responsibilities performed now by separate local governments. A regional government could include an entire metropolitan area that is now carved up into a variety of city, county, and district governments. It could have a broader revenue base and thus be more financially able to direct areawide programs. In addition, some problems, such as air pollution and transportation, require areawide planning and coordination for solution.

Advantages of Regional Government

Efficiency and better use of resources are usually the key points stressed by supporters of regional governments. Taxes would probably remain the same overall, but tax dollars would be more efficiently spent. If regional government were adopted, which local governments would be eliminated, and which retained? That is a difficult question, but it is clear that some existing levels must be retained to keep government close to local citizens. One advantage of the regional idea, however, is that such government would still be closer to an area's residents than, for instance, the state machinery, while gaining the efficiency of a larger body.

Some Beginnings

One suggestion is that a regional government be formed in the San Francisco area, to include the nine counties of the Bay region and the over 500 special districts and county and city governments there. The rather informal, loosely formed Association of Bay Area Governments has sometimes been thought of as a step in that direction, but it has never proved very effective. The Southern California Association of Governments has been more successful in attempting to coordinate a six-county area of southern California. But actual regional government has yet to be tried on a broad basis in California.

One move towards using the regional approach in a narrow, specific way is the previously discussed Porter–Cologne Water Quality Control Act, which established regional water control districts. Another is the work of the various Coastal Zone Commissions, which operate on a broad regional basis to preserve the coastline. Thus, California seems to be moving in the direction of regional government to accomplish specific objectives.[5]

Nonpartisanship

One of the important characteristics of California local government is its nonpartisan nature. At the local level, all judicial, county, city, and district offices are nonpartisan—that is, election campaigns for those positions are carried on with no party labels officially applied to candidates. To avoid the partisanship associated with traditional November election campaigns, city elections generally are held at other times during the year, usually in the spring.

The effort to divorce local government from partisan politics was a reform measure adopted early in this century. While many political observers have charged that nonpartisanship tends to produce weak, ineffective local governments, California voters generally seem enthusiastic, feeling that it has helped to prevent local corruption and avoid the conflicts, bickering, political dealing, and compromises traditionally associated with partisan politics.

Weakness of the Nonpartisan System

Critics of the nonpartisan idea think that election campaigns should focus on a candidate's approach to issues and his particular philosophy. They believe that when a label is applied to a candidate, his positions on issues are easier to identify. Under the present system, they say, campaigns tend to lack discussion of important issues, and stress personality more than ideas.

Furthermore, partisan local politics could provide financial backing to candidates who now lack a good funding base, because party treasuries could be opened to support less well-to-do candidates. Nonpartisan elections and campaigns traditionally have favored white, relatively affluent candidates. Partisan campaigns could open local politics to a broader range of candidates.[6]

Despite criticism, the nonpartisan nature of local politics has never been strongly challenged in California. No effort to introduce party politics into local government has gained widespread public support.

Lobbying and Special Interests

Because of the nonpartisan nature of local government, many people assume that special interest groups and lobbyists do not influence these officials. This is not true, although full-time professional lobbyists operate only in California's bigger cities. For example, in Los Angeles, which requires that lobbyists register with the city Clerk, some 398 individuals registered in the first three months of 1974. This situation, of course, is the exception, and the strongest pressures on city and county officials are usually the special interest groups. Many of these groups see their activity as highly informal and nonpolitical, and therefore, in keeping with the nonpartisan character of local affairs. Yet, they operate in a very political fashion.

Members of business and professional groups quite often are elected or appointed to the various boards and commissions. In some cities, for example, local businessmen and lawyers traditionally are elected to the city council. The local chamber of commerce, which represents business interests, is also able to make its position heard. Religious groups sometimes organize effective opposition, and ethnic groups have taken influential stands on such issues as housing and education.

Influencing Local Officials

How do these interests make their voices heard? If their members are not able to gain positions on boards and commissions, they must use a variety of means, including wide publicity, attendance at board meetings, and private meetings with public officials. These activities are as important to local government as to the state level. No matter how informal or well organized they may be, these lobbying activities are quite political. They can play a vital role in directing the efforts of local government.

Local Finances

Many times, lobbying activities are aimed at pressuring a local governing body to spend funds for a particular project. In California, as in other states, local government tax revenues are often insufficient to meet local needs. In fact, existing revenues often barely meet the expenses of current services, leaving no possibility of developing new facilities or services, no matter how desirable or badly needed they may be. Local governments find themselves in the awkward position of having a measure of self-rule, but being unable to finance their activities. They have had to look increasingly to state and federal monies to help them meet expenses, but sometimes find these sources drying up as well.

Importance of the Property Tax

The major finance problem for local governing bodies is that their revenue is tied primarily to the property tax. A single property tax bill may include a series of taxes assessed by the school system and other special districts as well as city and county government. This single tax represents the major source of income for all these bodies—one-third or more for cities and counties, and the total income for many districts. And, as local government costs rise, property taxes soar. Most tax reform ideas are aimed at finding relief for the overburdened property owner and uncovering a better way of financing local needs. Property taxes are considered unfair because they are not related to an owner's ability to pay (income), and therefore, they hit hardest persons who live on fixed or low incomes.

In addition to property tax income, state and federal funds provide substantial aid to local government—well over 40 percent of county income. Sales taxes also are quite important to cities in providing revenue. Almost one-half of a city's revenue base is composed of property and sales taxes.

The Watson Amendment and Reagan Initiative

In 1972 and 1973, much attention was focused on financing local government because of two proposed initiative amendments. First, the so-called Watson Initiative Amendment appeared on the November 1972 ballot. Supporters said that it would bring relief to the property owner as well as increase aid to local government. Critics charged that it was designed to benefit large land owners and a few special interests, would create disorder in local government financing, and would severely reduce school district income.

Shortly after voters defeated this measure, then-Governor Ronald Reagan opened his campaign for a revenue control and tax reduction initiative. Reagan's idea was to establish an effective means of controlling state revenues and expenses. Local governments became some of the measure's strongest critics. They discovered that if the state cut back programs and reduced spending as the initiative required, local governments would have to fund those programs, but that would be impossible because the initiative also intended to freeze property tax rates at the 1972 level. Local officials feared they would be completely unable to meet their needs. For these and other reasons, the Reagan Initiative also failed. But even though voters rejected them, both measures illustrated the continuing concern over controlling rapidly increasing property taxes in the face of ever-increasing local government needs.

The Need for Major Tax Reform

Major tax reform *is* needed. Despite complaints about soaring tax rates, present revenues do not keep up with expanding service needs or population growth, so any tax reform must include a way to expand revenues. One possible revenue source not currently used at the local level is the income tax, which is at least related to income and ability to pay, unlike the property tax. Property tax assessment also could be altered to reflect actual rather than potential use of land. And, as noted in Chapter Two, property taxes also might be changed to apply only to income-producing land, not to one's own home. Sales taxes also could be raised, applied differently, and used more to provide local revenues.

Regardless of which reforms are adopted, what is needed for local financing is a new tax base that can fund the rising cost of current programs, establish new services as they are needed, and deal with population growth. To accomplish all this without further overburdening taxpayers will require all the creativity and imagination experts can provide.

Environmental Issues

Local governments are heavily involved in environmental problems, often as a result of pressure from regional governing bodies. For example, the city of Santa Barbara has been in trouble with the Central Coast Water Quality Control Board over its old, outdated sewage treatment plant. For a while in 1972 a Board decision held up all new tie-ins to that sewage system until plant improvements were made. Some $7 million worth of building permits waited until the Board ban was lifted. The Central Valley Board has been concerned with Sacramento sewage disposal facilities. Board action forced the planning in 1973 of a countywide regional sewage disposal project to prevent further water contamination. In 1974, voters approved $75 million in bonds to begin upgrading local treatment plants, and that was only one-quarter of the total cost.

Another problem local governments have had to handle is that of open space and land use. As pointed out in Chapter Two, San Francisco became concerned enough with land use and open space in 1972 for its Board of Supervisors to enact strict limits and requirements on new planning and construction. These limits included placing height restrictions and bulk limits on construction.

Land use restrictions through tighter zoning and planning are being pushed by environmentalists, who see local growth rates threatening overuse of an area's resources. Retaining open space helps to slow down or at least redirect growth, and encourages solutions to the overuse of local resources. An earlier chapter described the work of both the city of Palo Alto and the Tahoe Regional Planning Agency, which used zoning provisions to regulate land use and prevent new growth from overburdening local government agencies. Palo Alto discovered that if its foothill areas were fully developed the city would face a heavy financial burden in attempting to provide and maintain the customary city services. To avoid that burden, the city zoned the area for open space.

Air pollution, noise pollution, and solid waste disposal are other environmental problems local governments are tackling. In a very real way, such issues are (or at least should be) more important to local governments than to any other level of government. The efforts of city and county governments to improve environmental quality can only aid in upgrading the local setting and making it a better place in which to live.

Minority Groups and Local Government

Another significant problem in local government is the lack of representation of minority views on appointed boards and commissions or on elected boards and councils. The nonpartisan nature of such groups has often preserved them for whites, and increasing political activism by minority groups has only partially changed the situation. In Sacramento, for instance, for 60 years members of the city council were elected at-large, rather than from specific districts of the city. The council customarily was made up of members who represented the downtown business establishment, were mostly white and well-to-do. Minority groups were rarely represented in council membership, and their needs and those of poorer city areas were somewhat ignored. In 1971, the election system was discarded and voters from each of eight districts began to elect their own representatives to the council. Only the mayor is elected at-large. As a result, the council makeup has changed noticeably. The downtown business establishment has ceased to control it, and minority representation has appeared in strength: among the members are a woman, an Asian, a Chicano, and a Black.

Disadvantages of Regional Government

In the San Francisco Bay area, where the push to form some kind of regional government is the strongest of any area within the state, a major problem is that minority groups foresee few benefits coming from such a regional operation. They believe regional government satisfies the needs of those who can afford to be concerned with air pollution, solid waste disposal, water pollution, and rapid transit. But many minority members, of necessity, are more concerned with jobs, education, and housing. They see regional government as simply a new way for well-to-do whites to establish firmer control over all local and regional development. The danger of regional government (at least in the Bay area) is that it may not only fail to deal with the real needs of minorities and of average citizens, but also may not even include them on its boards and commissions. Of course, to be effective regional government must have minority input. One concrete suggestion is that some regional government districts be purposely gerrymandered to preserve Black and Chicano communities.[7]

The Bobby Seale campaign for mayor of Oakland illustrates the differences that may exist between the white Establishment and minority group interests. As discussed before, Seale stressed the need for consumer protection, safe streets, taxing stocks and bonds, and a capital gains tax on local corporations. His objectives were basically social, and were designed to provide the city with funds that could be applied to programs to help the poor and minorities of Oakland. Seale's opponent, the incumbent mayor, discussed instead the need to attract industry to Oakland. Although that would have helped to accomplish some of Seale's objectives, the approaches of the two men were quite different, and showed the mayor's lack of interest in directly facing the problems of minorities.

Because minorities are underrepresented within local government they view it as an unresponsive institution. A major task of local government and any future regional governments is to open up to minority representation and participation. Only then can it be effective for all the people.

Reform Efforts

Despite the series of local issues crying for solutions, local government today remains divided, poorly financed, and unresponsive to the needs of minorities and the poor within its boundaries. Several kinds of reform have been suggested. For the Bay Area, a new regional government has been proposed. Los Angeles reformers support the idea of a county mayor and expanded membership on the Board of Supervisors. The need and purpose of many special districts should be reexamined. Perhaps both city and county government organizations are cluttered with traditional officers who are no longer needed, and new officers, roles, and responsibilities may be needed.

Updating the Government Structures

The need for reform or renovation has never been more vital. New problems have emerged that in total have overwhelmed local government—largely as a result of the great expansion of contemporary technology, economic growth, and urban concentration. Government organization set up on the needs of previous years—or previous centuries—is no longer able to resolve modern problems. Urban decline, pollution, urban sprawl, and welfare and medical assistance responsibilities are among the enormous problems requiring fresh solutions.

Two problems in particular may illustrate the basic nature of the challenge facing local government. As pointed out in Chapter Two, the challenge of proper land use often includes more than just a single city or county; an effective policy must focus on a large area and its needs. Local laws and policies have tended to confuse and limit efforts to obtain better land management, agricultural and urban policy on land use, and state land planning. A regional or statewide perspective on land use is necessary to handle air pollution, water pollution, subdivision planning, and the preservation of agricultural areas. Local governments cannot successfully handle the task.

The problem of public transportation furnishes another example of the advantages of having a regional approach and the inadequate resources of local government. An areawide solution is required in most cases to assure both adequate financing and actual use of the system. To establish a coordinated plan, intertwining highways, bus systems, and a fixed rail transit operation, demands a regional and perhaps statewide approach.

Changing Roles

These problems and others suggest a growing inadequacy of local government to solve community problems. The roles of federal, state, and local government are no longer well defined. New problems that call for solutions beyond the reach of local government have required the increased participation of both federal and state agencies.

The future of local government lies in rethinking many traditional responsibilities—solving revenue problems by searching out an adequate revenue base, handling environmental and land use problems much more effectively, and taking a new look at the structure of local government.

Lack of Voter Interest

One other vital problem needs attention as well: how to make local government more interesting to the average Californian. If voting records are any indication, Californians are almost completely disinterested in most local elections. Only when controversial issues or people are involved do voters make an effort to go to the polls. This situation suggests a need for a means of encouraging more interest in local government, in addition to reforms in structure and financing. The fact that California voters are continually more interested in state-level elections than in local ones may mean they feel closer to state government than to local government. Much remains to be done to upgrade local government and to convince most Californians that it is important and responsive and interested in their needs and problems.[8]

Review Questions

What types of county government exist in California? In what ways do they differ?

What are the responsibilities of the Board of Supervisors?

What does a chief administrator do?

Name some of the important county officials.

How is authority and responsibility fragmented in county government?

What are some of the services county government provides?

Name the two types of mayors found in California city governments, and describe the differences between them.

What is the difference between the mayor–council form of government and the council–manager form?

What are some of the services city government provides?

What is a special district? What functions do such districts have? What tax powers do they have?

How would you define regional government? Is regional government being used in California?

Which tax is the major source of income for local government? Why is it a burden?

What problems do minority groups have in working with local government?

Notes

1. A most helpful and very concise description of county government is Jane Gladfelder, *California's Emergent Counties* (County Supervisors Association of California, 1968). This is available from the County Supervisors' Association office in Sacramento. This Association also publishes a *California County Fact Book* each year.

2. Reed McClure, "Why Everyone Wants to Be Supervisor," *California Journal* 5 (January, 1974): 26–27. This presents an interesting discussion of the position of Los Angeles County Supervisor.

3. Warren Olney, "Mayor Bradley's Quest for 'Leadership,' " *California Journal* 5 (January, 1974): 22–25. Los Angeles *Times,* June 30, 1974.

4. Information on California cities can be easily obtained from the League

of California Cities, which has offices in Sacramento and Los Angeles.

5. Randall Shores, "Regional Government: Its Structure, Functions, and Finance," *California Journal* 4 (January, 1973): 15–21. This article, written basically to answer the question, "What is Regional Government?" is a good survey treatment.

6. Robert L. Morlan and Leroy C. Hardy have a fine discussion of this in their book, *Politics in California* (Belmont: Dickenson Publishing Co., 1968), chapter 6.

7. The suggestion for minority districts through the gerrymandering approach came from Assemblyman Willie L. Brown, Jr., at the 1968 Conference on Bay Area Regional Organization. Further minority problems with regional government were explored by Donald P. McCullum at the 1970 conference on the same subject. See Harriet Nathan and Stanley Scott, ed., *Toward a Bay Area Regional Organization* (Berkeley: Institute of Governmental Studies, 1969), pp. 84–98, and Stanley Scott and Harriet Nathan, ed., *Adapting Government to Regional Needs* (Berkeley: Institute of Governmental Studies, 1971), pp. 146–151.

8. Reagan's Task Force on Local Government Reform issued a very provocative report in July, 1974. It was basically a defense of much of the status quo, including the vast number of special districts. While more flexibility was called for within the local government setting, regional government was viewed as a hazard to responsive and effective local governing bodies. Interestingly, Reagan apparently disagreed with the Task Force Report and did not sign it.

CHAPTER EIGHT

CHANGE: THE PATTERN OF THE FUTURE

What does the future hold for California? Change. That is California government's greatest challenge. If government is to remain effective, find solutions to the problems of the state, and meet the needs of *all* Californians, it must meet that challenge.

Instead of thinking about California as a single unit, you must recognize the remarkable differences within her borders. An uncommon and wonderful mix of varying opinions, ideas, needs, and demands springs from her separate areas. In election after election Californians from various state regions clearly reveal major philosophical differences.

One of the few forces that has brought a sense of unity is government. Historically, artificial links in the form of roads, railroads, and airline transportation have brought all areas into contact with one another. Yet it has been left to government to bring a better feeling of unity through working to find solutions to Californians' problems.

At the turn of this century political corruption was widespread at both state and local governmental levels. In response to this situation, a strong political reform movement appeared. Those reformers gave California nonpartisan elections, the direct primary, recall, initiative and referendum procedures, and other vitally needed tools. And the reform movement provided unity.

What brings unity today? A similar need to improve government. A statewide need exists to face certain issues and find answers. For example, statewide problems include the necessity for greater involvement of minorities in the government process. Air pollution and water pollution problems can be solved only through coordinated efforts. Better methods of financing for school districts and local government are a pressing need. Furthermore, solutions must be found to local government problems of fragmentation, unresponsiveness, and the lack of citizen interest.

While it is important to see the statewide nature of these problems and the demand for wide-range solutions, it is equally important to realize that these problems have an unusual characteristic: they are constantly changing. A good example of this can be found in the government efforts to meet state water needs. Since the late nineteenth century, Californians have supported the building of many water projects to bring water to dry areas and to end the danger of floods. Just a decade ago, public support of these efforts was widespread and unquestioned. But in the period of the late 1960s and early 1970s environmentalists began an attack on the newest project. They pointed out the great damage being done by the project. Are the benefits worth that damage?

A similar change has hit freeway building. Since the beginning of this century, Californians have pushed road building. In the early 1970s, however, that changed. A new demand appeared: the planning of alternate modes of transportation. In 1973 a new Department of Transportation began operation to plan balanced statewide transportation systems.

Why then is change the greatest challenge facing California government? Because it is government's only constant challenge. For example, the need for water planning will remain, but the approach to solving that problem will change. Thus, the greatest single characteristic that California government requires is the ability to adjust to change at all levels. If government meets that challenge, it succeeds. If it does not, it will fail California's world. In the early 1970s, state government showed its ability to meet change; local government did not. Consequently, the major task now seems to be: finding ways to make California local government more responsive to changing needs. Otherwise, the state will gradually take over local duties and responsibilities and shove aside local government.

How can California government remain responsive? It must maintain a sense of openness in meeting the changing needs of the state. It must be willing to alter its procedures, planning, and maybe some parts of its structure to do so. Local government, for example, may need to be restructured in some areas to keep abreast of change. California government must be flexible and adaptable.

As stressed before, government is a process in action. Citizens exercise political power and make their wills known through government. Government expresses the will of the majority. Government as a process, therefore, must remain open, responsive, and sensitive to minority opinion on all subjects. If this is continually achieved, government will adapt to changing needs, and reform will maintain itself as a continuing process. The challenge of constant change will then be met.

Change is the pattern of California's future. Government must be prepared to meet that pattern if it is to survive effectively.

INDEX